Ida B. Wells

Ida B. Wells

Mother of the Civil Rights Movement

Dennis Brindell Fradin
and Judith Bloom Fradin

CLARION BOOKS

New York

Clarion Books
a Houghton Mifflin Company imprint
215 Park Avenue South, New York, NY 10003
Copyright © 2000 by Dennis Brindell Fradin and Judith Bloom Fradin

The text for this book was set in 14-pt. Dante
Book design by Carol Goldenberg
Picture research by Judith Bloom Fradin

Library of Congress Cataloging-in-Publication Data
Fradin, Dennis B.
Ida B. Wells : mother of the civil rights movement /
by Dennis Brindell Fradin and Judith Bloom Fradin.
p. cm.
Includes bibliographical references (p.169) and index.
ISBN 0-395-89898-6
1. Wells-Barnett, Ida B., 1862–1931 Juvenile literature. 2. Afro-American
women civil rights workers Biography Juvenile literature. 3. Civil rights
workers—United States Biography Juvenile literature. 4. Afro-American
women journalists Biography Juvenile literature. 5. Lynching—United
States—History Juvenile literature. 6. United States—Race relations
Juvenile literature.
I. Fradin, Judith Bloom. II. Title.
E185.97.W55F73   2000
323'.092—dc21
[B]   99-37038
CIP

VB 10 9 8 7 6 5

For our dear grandson,
Aaron Bernard Todd Fradin, with love

For their gracious assistance, the authors thank Donald Duster,
Benjamin Duster, and Alfreda Duster Ferrell,
grandchildren of Ida B. Wells-Barnett

Contents

Ida B. Wells in about 1893

A Note from the Authors

OF ALL THE GREAT civil rights leaders, Ida B. Wells is one of the least known—yet one of the most important.

Most people know that by refusing to relinquish her seat to a white passenger on an Alabama bus in 1955, Rosa Parks helped end segregation in public places in the United States. Yet few realize that seventy-one years earlier, in 1884, Ida B. Wells fought a similar battle by refusing to give up her seat in a "Whites Only" train car in Tennessee. It took three men to drag the twenty-one-year-old schoolteacher from the train, and all the influence the railroad could summon to defeat her subsequent lawsuit.

Most people also know that during the 1950s and 1960s, Dr. Martin Luther King Jr. led the struggle for black people to obtain justice in the fields of education, jobs, and housing. Yet few people know that Ida B. Wells led similar struggles as far back as the 1890s. Among her many achievements, she helped create the National Association for the Advancement of Colored People (NAACP), which still works for the rights of black people and other minorities.

Susan B. Anthony is remembered for leading the campaign for women's voting rights. Ida B. Wells was a leader in that movement, too. She created the Alpha Suffrage Club, one of the country's first organizations to work for the right of black women to vote.

Wells was noteworthy in many other ways. A prominent journalist, she owned and edited a newspaper in her hometown of Memphis, Tennessee. In Chicago she founded the Negro Fellowship League, a neighborhood center that helped hundreds of poor people find jobs. When funds for the center dwindled, Wells became Chicago's first female probation officer, and donated much of her salary to the center, keeping it going for ten years. She managed all this while raising six children with her husband, Ferdinand Barnett, a lawyer and newspaperman, to whom she was married for thirty-six years.

This is quite a list of accomplishments for a woman born a slave, but it only begins to tell the story of Ida B. Wells, or Ida B. Wells-Barnett, as she was called after her marriage. In one crucial area of the civil rights movement she was the undisputed leader. Thousands of southern black people were lynched—hanged, shot, or burned to death by mobs without a trial—in the late 1800s and early 1900s. In 1892 three black men in Memphis, including her friend Thomas Moss, were lynched—simply because they ran a more successful grocery store than a white neighbor's. Enraged by the murders, Ida decided to do something.

She visited places where lynchings had occurred, spoke to the victims' relatives, and corresponded with witnesses. She discovered that black people were routinely lynched for such alleged offenses as horse stealing, barn burning, and "talking sassy" to white people. In many cases the lynching victims had been falsely accused but were hunted down because bloodthirsty mobs wanted to kill any black person they could find. Law officers often refused to protect the victims and sometimes participated in the murders. At times, newspapers incited the lynchings, and even announced where and when they would occur in order to attract huge crowds. Incredibly, state governors sometimes knew about upcoming lynchings but refused to stop them. The worst part, Wells realized, was that lynching victims were deprived of the "right to a speedy and public trial," guaranteed to all Americans by the Bill of Rights.

Wells wrote articles describing the horrors of lynching, insisting that

Artist's version of the lynching horror

the perpetrators be arrested "in the name of God and in the name of the law we have always upheld." Angered by her writings, a white mob broke into her office in Memphis and destroyed it. Fortunately Wells was out of town, or she might have joined the list of lynching victims. She never could live in Memphis again, for a number of the city's white men threatened to kill her on sight if she returned.

Ida moved north and continued her campaign against lynching. She wrote powerful works on the subject, including *Southern Horrors* and *A Red Record*. She traveled extensively in the United States and abroad to speak against lynching, and met with at least two presidents of the United States. Thanks largely to Ida's work, lynching in the United States was nearly wiped out by the time of her death in 1931.

One reason Ida B. Wells is not better known is that she was militantly outspoken at a time when black people were expected to "know their place." She advised black people to fight back against oppression and bought herself a pistol after Thomas Moss's murder. "I felt that one had better die fighting against injustice than die like a rat in a trap," Ida declared in her autobiography, *Crusade for Justice*. She accused readers who did nothing to stop lynching of being part of the problem. "Men and women of America, are you proud of this record [of lynching]?" she wrote in her pamphlet *Mob Rule in New Orleans*. "Your silence seems to say that you are. Only by earnest, active, united endeavor to arouse public sentiment can we hope to put a stop to these demonstrations of American barbarism." She made black people almost as uncomfortable as she made white people. Several times black leaders asked Ida to "soft-pedal" her criticisms. Wells refused and, by so doing, became the most militant voice of black protest of her time and the spiritual mother of our country's civil rights movement.

Ida's greatest admirers were the many people whose lives she saved by her "crusade for justice." All of us who live in what she called "this land of the free and home of the brave" should thank Ida B. Wells for saving us from what has been called our national crime—the evil of lynching.

—D.B.F & J.B.F.

Ida B.Wells

Ida B. Wells at about the time she visited the condemned men in Arkansas

"Let Your Prayers Be Songs of Faith and Hope"

O N A SUNDAY in January 1922, a group of black women walked into a prison in Little Rock, Arkansas, to visit twelve inmates. All but one of the visitors were the prisoners' wives or mothers. Had prison officials known the name of the short, heavyset, gray-haired woman with penetrating eyes, they wouldn't have allowed her inside. To keep the woman's identity secret, one of the prisoners' wives, a Mrs. Moore, told the officials that the stranger was her cousin from St. Louis.

A guard led the women to the cells of the prisoners, who were under a sentence of death. As the women greeted their loved ones, the guard settled into a chair about fifty feet from the cells and read the Sunday newspaper. "Boys," Mrs. Moore said, loud enough for the guard to hear, "come and shake hands with my cousin who has come from St. Louis to see me."

One by one the prisoners approached the bars of their cells to shake hands with the short woman. As they did so, Mrs. Moore whispered, "This is Mrs. Barnett from Chicago." Looks of joy spread across the faces of the condemned men. All twelve had heard of the civil rights worker Ida B. Wells-Barnett, and one man had written the letter asking her to investigate their case. Seeing their reaction to her presence, Ida B. Wells put a finger to her lips as a signal for them not to mention her real name.

The story of these twelve condemned men is a sad commentary on American society in the early 1900s. They and their families had been sharecroppers—farmers who lived on other people's land, sharing a portion of their crops with the landowners in lieu of rent. Southern sharecroppers were paid low prices for their crops and generally lived in extreme poverty. In Phillips County, Arkansas, along the Mississippi River, sharecroppers had tried to join together into a union to demand better prices for their cotton. Outraged by the idea of poor black farmers demanding *anything,* armed gangs of white ruffians from Arkansas, Tennessee, and Mississippi poured into Phillips County and murdered dozens of black sharecroppers.

Instead of arresting the murderers, the authorities jailed hundreds of black men and women for planning a "revolt" and for conspiring to murder white people. In a mockery of a trial that lasted just a few minutes, the all-white jury found nearly one hundred black people guilty as charged. Sixty-seven of them were sentenced to long prison terms, and twelve were condemned to death.

Ida B. Wells spoke quietly to one man after another. They told her that since being moved to the prison in Little Rock, the capital of Arkansas, they had been treated fairly well, but earlier, in the jails of Phillips County, they had suffered constant torment. A lynch mob had tried to break into a jail to seize them. They had been beaten and given electric shocks until they confessed to having plotted to "kill white folks." Three times they had nearly been executed, only to be saved by last-minute appeals to the courts.

Wells asked the men to describe their farms and union, the massacre by the whites, and details of their trial and imprisonment. She had to remember what they said, because taking notes would have been risky. Previously, a civil rights worker who had tried to interview the men while posing as a newspaper reporter had been discovered and nearly lynched. For Ida B. Wells the danger was especially intense. Thirty years earlier she had been exiled from the South because an article she had written about lynching had antagonized white people. This was probably Ida's first trip back south since then, yet plenty of people who recalled what she had written in 1892 and who knew of her subsequent work would have relished the prospect of running her out of town or lynching her.

Once Wells had all the information she needed, Mrs. Moore said, "Boys, don't you want to sing for my cousin?" The men then sang several religious songs called spirituals, one of which they had composed. As the men sang about heaven and the wonderful life they expected in the hereafter, the warden overheard them. He came in to listen, accompanied by his wife and their dinner guests. When the singing ended, the warden and his wife and their guests returned to their dinner, and the prisoners looked to Ida B. Wells for approval. Instead they saw anger in her eyes.

Standing near the bars of their cells, she told them in a low voice, "I have listened to you for nearly two hours. You have talked and sung and prayed about dying, and forgiving your enemies, and of feeling sure

Participants in the Phillips County riot; they are believed to be the twelve condemned men whose lives Ida B. Wells helped save.

you are going to be received in heaven because you are innocent of the offense for which you expect to be electrocuted. But why don't you pray to live and ask to be freed? Let all your songs and prayers be songs of faith and hope that God will set you free. Quit talking about dying. If you believe God is all-powerful, believe he is powerful enough to open these prison doors. Dying is the last thing you ought to think about, much less talk about. Pray to live and believe you are going to get out."

Wells left the prison with the rest of the women. She stayed up nearly all night writing down what the men and their wives and mothers had told her, as best she could remember.

After returning by train to Chicago, she turned her notes into a pamphlet called *The Arkansas Race Riot,* which described the unjust treatment of the black sharecroppers from Phillips County. She raised money to print a thousand copies, many of which she sent to influential people in Arkansas. Thanks in part to Wells's efforts, in 1923 the Supreme Court of the United States ruled that the twelve condemned men had not received a fair trial. All of them were freed.

One Sunday evening around Christmas of 1923, Ida B. Wells came home to find a well-dressed young man waiting at her door. "Good evening, Mrs. Barnett," he said with extreme politeness. "Do you know who I am?"

"I do not," she said, not quite able to place him.

"I am one of the twelve men that you came down to Arkansas about last year." He had recently moved to Chicago, he explained, and had been searching for her to thank her.

Ida B. Wells went inside with the young man and introduced him to her family.

"Mrs. Barnett told us to quit talking about dying, that we ought to pray to God to open our prison doors," he said. "After that, we never talked about dying anymore, but did as she told us, and now every last one of us is out and enjoying his freedom."

"A Butterfly Schoolgirl"

IDA BELL WELLS was born a slave on July 16, 1862, during the conflict that killed more Americans than any other war in history. Her birthplace was Holly Springs, Mississippi, but the country Mississippi belonged to at the time was a matter of opinion, as was the name of the war and the reasons for fighting it.

White southerners considered Mississippi to be part of the Confederate States of America, comprising eleven southern states that had joined together in 1861 after withdrawing from the United States of America. That year the Confederacy had gone to war against the United States, also called the Union, which was composed mainly of the northern states. Claiming they were fighting to protect states' rights—including their right to continue slavery—southerners called the conflict the War of Northern Aggression. Northerners, on the other hand, considered the Confederacy an illegal government. Asserting that they were fighting to end slavery and keep the United States one nation, northerners called the conflict the War of Southern Rebellion. Today most Americans call it the Civil War.

Ida was the first child of Elizabeth and James Wells, slaves on the Bolling farm in Holly Springs. As the child of slaves, Ida was automatically a slave, too, from the moment of her birth. She did not belong to her parents but to the Bollings. James Wells worked as a handyman and carpenter for Mr. Bolling, while Elizabeth Wells was the Bollings' cook.

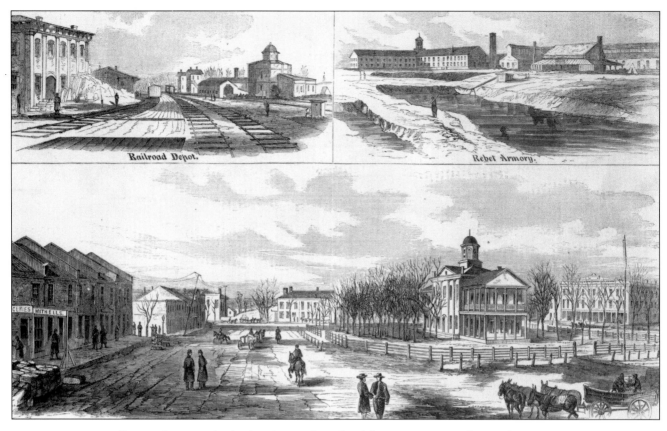

Holly Springs, Mississippi, as sketched by an artist when Ida was about six months old

Had the war not changed things, Ida probably would have also been brought up as a cook for the white family.

As a small child, Ida must have become accustomed to the sound of gunfire and horses galloping through town. The North and the South both considered Holly Springs a strategic point. During the four years of the war, northern troops raided the town approximately sixty times. For a while Holly Springs was headquarters for Ulysses S. Grant, a northern general who later became the eighteenth president of the United States.

The slaves were freed in Holly Springs in August 1862, when Ida was only one month old. However, not until the North won the Civil War in the spring of 1865 were southern slaves guaranteed their freedom. Not quite three years old, Ida did not know why her parents were so happy, but over the next few years her understanding grew.

Like many other ex-slave families, the Wellses stayed on for a time with their former owners, only they received wages and were free to leave whenever they chose. Trouble soon developed between Ida's father and Mr. Bolling. Black men in Mississippi were allowed to vote for the first time in 1867. (American women, white and black, didn't win the vote until many years later.) In the years following the Civil War black people generally favored the Republicans, the party of Abraham Lincoln and the party that had freed the slaves. Mr. Bolling ordered James Wells to vote for the Democratic Party, which at that time included many white people who had favored slavery. Reminding Mr. Bolling that slavery was over, Ida's father declared that he would vote as he pleased. James Wells did what he said, but upon his return from the polling place he found that his family was no longer welcome in the little cabin on the Bolling property. James Wells soon rented another house in Holly Springs for his family and opened his own carpentry business in town.

After Ida, seven more children were born to Elizabeth and James

Cotton has long been grown in the Holly Springs area.

Black men voting just after the Civil War

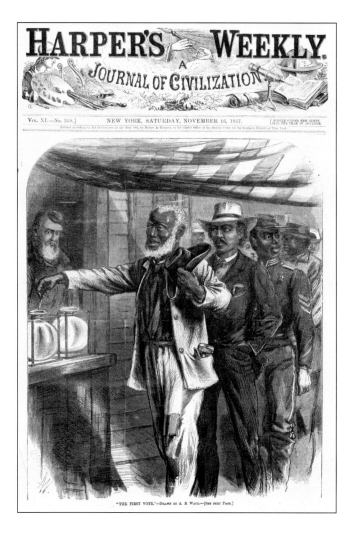

Wells. As the oldest, Ida often had to watch over her brothers and sisters. Each Saturday night her job was to bathe all of them and get their clothes and shoes ready for Sunday church. Ida especially helped care for her sister Eugenia, who had been paralyzed by a childhood illness and could not walk.

Elizabeth and James Wells could not read, for it had been a serious crime to educate slaves in the South. So instead of reading to her children, Elizabeth Wells told them true stories of her experiences in slavery. She described her separation from her parents at the age of seven and how some of her owners had beaten her. Ida's father disliked discussing slave days, but Ida once overheard him talking to his mother—Ida's grand-mother. "Jim," Grandmother Peggy Wells had said, "my old mistress, Miss Polly, wants you to come and bring the children. She wants to see them."

"Mother," Ida's father replied, "I never want to see that old woman as long as I live. I'll never forget how she had you stripped and whipped, and I will never see her. I guess it is all right for you to take care of her and forgive her for what she did to you, but she could have starved to death if I'd had my say-so!"

Following the Civil War, an office of the U.S. government called the Freedmen's Bureau, as well as a number of other agencies, opened schools for black people throughout the South. In 1866, what would become Rust College was founded in Holly Springs. In its early days the school taught ex-slaves of all ages, from young children to old people. As one of the most respected members of Holly Springs's black community, Ida's father was named a trustee of the school, but he apparently never learned to read or write. Ida's mother attended school with her children until she was able to read her Bible. She then withdrew from school but continued to visit her children's classes regularly to check on their progress.

By the age of about six, Ida could read very well. One of her earliest memories was of reading the newspaper aloud to her father and an admiring group of his friends. Sometimes she overheard her father and his friends talking about the Ku Klux Klan. Although she didn't under-stand what the Klan was, she recalled in her autobiography that "I knew dimly that it meant something fearful, by the anxious way my mother walked the floor at night when my father was out at a political meeting."

Ida's parents did their best to shield their children from the hatred many southern whites felt toward the ex-slaves. Before readmission to the Union, the southern states had to undergo a period called Recon-struction, during which they were forced to grant black people their rights. For a time black men could vote in the South while many white

Ida could be one of the pupils in this photograph showing the school associated with Rust College in about 1870.

men couldn't, resulting in the election of the region's first black lawmakers. In 1870, Mississippi's Hiram Rhodes Revels, who lived part of his life in Holly Springs, became the first black U.S. senator. Southern blacks held many other offices in the first years after the Civil War.

Resenting their former slaves' success, some white southerners formed hate groups, such as the Ku Klux Klan, that terrorized and murdered black people. White bigots murdered approximately five thousand southern blacks in 1865–66. Hundreds more were slain in race riots. In 1866 a white mob swept through Memphis, Tennessee, murdering about fifty black men, women, and children and wounding dozens of others during a three-day rampage. One of the victims was Robert Reed Church, a wealthy and respected property owner and bank founder. Church was warned that because he was black, he would be shot if he entered his own saloon. He went anyway and was shot in the head—by white policemen who stole his money. Church survived, but this man who would later come to the rescue of Ida B. Wells and the entire city of Memphis suffered from terrible headaches the rest of his life.

It appears that Ida's father belonged to a black voting rights organization

Ku Klux Klan members wearing disguises and burning a cross while spreading their message of hatred

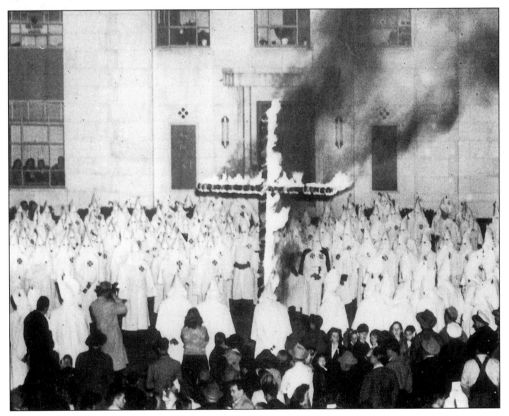

HARPER'S WEEKLY.

JOURNAL OF CIVILIZATION

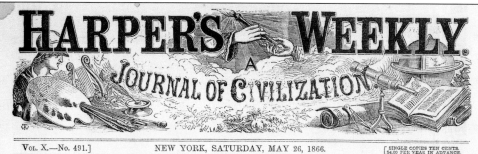

VOL. X.—No. 491.] NEW YORK, SATURDAY, MAY 26, 1866. [SINGLE COPIES TEN CENTS. $4.00 PER YEAR IN ADVANCE.

Entered according to Act of Congress, in the Year 1866, by Harper & Brothers, in the Clerk's Office of the District Court for the Southern District for New York.

THE MEMPHIS RIOTS.

THERE was in Memphis, on the first two days of May, an excitement unequalled since the close of the war. The origin of the disturbance between the whites and negroes of that city was highly discreditable to the colored soldiers, and the riotous proceedings which followed were a disgrace to civilization. For the riot the lower class of white citizens were as responsible as were the soldiers of the Third United States Colored Infantry for the original difficulty. This regiment, whose reputation has been a bad one, had been mustered out, since which they had frequented whisky-shops in the southern part of the city, and had been guilty of excesses and disorderly conduct. On the evening of May 1 some drunken members of the regiment were on South Street, talking noisily, when in an insolent manner they were ordered by two policemen to cease their noise and disperse. Words ensued, followed by blows, throwing of missiles, and firing of revolvers.

To understand what followed it must be remembered that the police force of Memphis is composed mostly of Irishmen, whose violent prejudice against negroes was so shamefully displayed in the New York riots of 1863. The *Times* correspondent thus described the riot:

Ward was sent to police head-quarters, and the whole force at once proceeded to the scene of the fray, being joined on the way thither by armed and excited citizens. Meanwhile the firing had brought other negroes to the spot, some armed with clubs and some with revolvers, so that by the time the police force came up the two parties were about equal in number. The negroes held the original

position, and, upon the approach of the police, showing no determination to abandon it, were fired upon by the police and citizens who accompanied them. This fire was returned, and for a while both parties busied themselves in discharging their revolvers as rapidly as possible. Meanwhile word was sent to General STONEMAN, who promptly despatched to the scene of action a company of Regulars (white), when the negroes were quickly dispersed and driven in every direction.

During the evening the wildest and most exaggerated reports soon spread throughout the city. Every communicator of the intelligence of the fight told a different story, and the highest excitement prevailed. Each rumor placed a worse aspect upon the affair than the preceding one, and only served to develop the pent-up prejudices against the negro. Soon after dark this excitement and prejudice found vent. Large numbers of armed citizens repaired to the scene of the fight and commenced firing upon every negro who made himself visible. One negro upon South Street, a quiet, inoffensive laborer, was shot down almost in front of his own cabin, and after life was extinct his body was fired into, cut and beat in a most horrible manner. In all parts of the city, wherever they could be seen, negroes were fired upon by policemen as well as citizens. They were shot while driving hacks, and quietly walking in the streets about their business. The police seemed to make it their special business to shoot every negro they could see, no matter where he was or what he was doing. The result was that by 9 o'clock the colored population were in-doors trembling with wild alarm. How many negroes were killed during the night it is impossible to ascertain, as firing was constantly heard during the earlier hours in all parts of the city. It is estimated that from 15 to 20 were killed. So far as I have been able to learn, not a white man was fired upon by a negro during the whole night.

After the fight of Tuesday evening the negro soldiers and most of the colored population residing in the vicinity of the fight fled to the fort for security. They were perfectly quiet—in fact, were terribly frightened for their own safety. At an early hour yesterday morning every thing

SCENES IN MEMPHIS, TENNESSEE, DURING THE RIOT—BURNING A FREEDMEN'S SCHOOL-HOUSE.

[SKETCHED BY A. R. W.]

SCENES IN MEMPHIS, TENNESSEE, DURING THE RIOT—SHOOTING DOWN NEGROES ON THE MORNING OF MAY 2, 1866.—[SKETCHED BY A. R. W.]

called the Loyal League. James Wells may have been present when the Ku Klux Klan raided a Loyal League meeting with the intention of shooting a white man who was informing black people of their voting rights. Fortunately the shot missed, but the meeting was broken up by the raid.

Despite such incidents, Ida enjoyed a pleasant and rather peaceful childhood in Holly Springs. Many years later she referred to herself during this period as "a happy, light-hearted schoolgirl" and "a butterfly schoolgirl." She was treated like a princess at home. She loved school, earned top grades, and read every book she could find, including the entire Bible and all of Shakespeare's plays. Louisa May Alcott's *Little Women* and such Charles Dickens classics as *A Christmas Carol* and *Oliver Twist* were among her other favorites. During the summertime Ida and other family members visited Grandmother Peggy Wells on her farm far out in the Mississippi countryside.

Ida celebrated her sixteenth birthday on July 16, 1878. At about that time she went to visit Grandmother Peggy for summer vacation. Ida was at her grandmother's farm when a yellow fever epidemic broke out in Memphis, fifty miles from Holly Springs, and in Grenada, Mississippi, eighty miles from Ida's home. An infectious disease of warm regions, yellow fever is carried by mosquitoes. At the time, however, it was believed to be carried by "swamp vapor." Since Holly Springs stood on relatively high ground, it was thought that yellow fever wouldn't strike there. The mayor and other officials of Holly Springs decided to allow people fleeing Memphis and Grenada into their town.

That was a terrible mistake. Yellow fever, so named because it turns the skin yellow, broke out in Holly Springs. Most of the town's thirty-five hundred people fled. Of the fifteen hundred people who remained in Holly Springs, all but about sixty contracted the disease. The Marshall County courthouse in Holly Springs was filled with cots and transformed into a hospital, while the lawn outside the courthouse was stacked with coffins and turned into a morgue.

Grandmother Peggy's farm was so far out in the country that newspapers were unavailable and mail delivery was slow. Ida heard about the epidemic gripping her town without knowing its severity. Moreover, she assumed that her parents had left with the children to stay with relatives outside Holly Springs. In fact, James and Elizabeth Wells remained in Holly Springs with Ida's brothers and sisters to help tend the sick. Besides caring for their own children, Elizabeth prepared food for stricken families, while Jim made coffins for the dead. Late that summer the disease struck the Wells household.

Still confident that her family had fled Holly Springs, Ida waited for news on her grandmother's farm. One day in early fall, while her grandmother, aunt, and uncle were out picking cotton in the field, Ida saw three men on horseback ride up to the gate. Recognizing them as

Gravediggers at work during the yellow fever epidemic of 1878

friends of her parents' from Holly Springs, Ida invited them inside and asked for news from home. One of the men handed her a letter a neighbor had written:

> Jim and Lizzie Wells have both died of the fever. They died within 24 hours of each other. The children are all at home and the Howard Association has put a woman there to take care of them. Send word to Ida.

At sixteen Ida had lost both her parents in the epidemic. She had no time to mourn, for she knew she had to return home to care for her brothers and sisters, who might also be ill. Grandmother Peggy argued that it would be too dangerous for Ida to enter an area where so many people were sick, but after several days she finally relented.

No passenger trains were running to Holly Springs, for it was dangerous to enter the stricken town. Only freight trains were going there. When a freight train pulled into the station nearest Grandmother Peggy's farm, bystanders begged Ida not to step aboard. The train conductor explained that the caboose was draped in black to honor two previous conductors who had died of yellow fever. If Ida returned home, the conductor warned, she would probably succumb to the disease. "I am the oldest of seven living children. There's nobody but me to look after them now," Ida answered, boarding the black-draped caboose.

Even the freight train wouldn't approach closer than three miles to Holly Springs, so Ida probably walked the last part of the trip. When she reached home, she discovered that her brother Stanley, only nine months old, was among the 304 Holly Springs people who died in the epidemic. (Another brother, Eddie, had died years earlier.) That left five brothers and sisters for Ida to care for. All of them but Eugenia had contracted yellow fever, but their cases were less severe than their parents' and Stanley's had been, and they were recovering.

The Howard Association, a forerunner of the American Red Cross, had sent a nurse to assist the Wells family. Ida fortunately did not contract yellow fever, and she helped care for her sisters and brothers until they all recovered. Around the time of Halloween of 1878, the epidemic finally ended.

James Wells had been a member of a fraternal group called the Masons. Although most Masons were white, a black man named Prince Hall had organized the first Masonic lodge for African Americans in the late 1700s. Black Masonic lodges spread throughout the country, including Holly Springs. James Wells's Masonic lodge brothers were expected to protect his orphaned children. One Sunday afternoon in November the lodge brothers and their wives arrived at the Wells house to decide what to do with Ida and her sisters and brothers.

Ida listened as her parents' friends discussed her family's future. The wives of two Masons wanted to raise five-year-old Annie and two-year-old Lily. Two of the men thought that eleven-year-old James and nine-year-old George had inherited their father's skill with tools and wanted to adopt them and train them as carpenters. Ida was considered old enough to fend for herself. Because no one offered crippled Eugenia a home, she was to be sent to the poorhouse.

Ida waited until they were finished and then spoke up. She thanked her parents' friends for their concern, but announced: "You are not going to put any of the children anywhere. It would make my father and mother turn over in their graves to know their children had been scattered. We own our house, and if you will help me find work, I will take care of my brothers and sisters."

The adults scoffed at the prospect of a sixteen-year-old girl raising five children, but Ida wouldn't budge. According to family legend, Ida grabbed a shotgun off a shelf and threatened the lodge brothers with it so they would know she meant business. Two of the men, James Hall and Bob Miller, had been appointed as the children's guardians. Mr. Hall and Mr. Miller made a deal with Ida. At the time, rural areas had so great a need for teachers that young people who could pass a test were often hired to teach. If Ida could pass the country schoolteacher's examination, she could take charge of her brothers and sisters.

Besides the house, James and Elizabeth Wells had left their children three hundred dollars, equivalent to about six thousand dollars today. The family lived on those funds while Ida prepared for and passed the teacher's test. She was assigned to a school for black children six miles out in the country. Traveling between her school and Holly Springs was difficult, so Ida arranged to live at the schoolhouse or with her students' families during the week and to return home on weekends. Grandmother Peggy Wells moved into the house in Holly Springs to care for her grandchildren during the week while Ida was away.

Ida lengthened her dresses and pulled her hair into a bun to make herself appear older than sixteen. Each Sunday night she rode out to her one-room school on the back of a big white mule in order to be ready for class Monday morning. On Friday afternoon she rode the six miles home on the mule. All day Saturday and Sunday she washed, ironed, and cooked for her brothers and sisters. Then she graded her students' work.

Teaching was much more difficult than Ida had anticipated. She was barely older than some of her students, which made maintaining discipline a challenge. Not only that, but life was becoming more difficult for the ex-slaves in every way. Reconstruction had ended in 1877. As white southerners regained control of their governments, they took away the rights of black people. For one thing, separate schools for black and white children were established throughout the South. Schools for black students, like the one where Ida B. Wells taught, had no books, paper, or supplies except what the teacher brought.

Whites also stripped black citizens of their right to vote. One tactic was to charge a poll tax—a fee people had to pay to cast their ballot. But even if blacks could afford the poll tax, white people had other ways to keep them from voting. Constitution tests were given at many polling places. In order to vote, a man had to explain a part of the U.S. Constitution.

School in South Carolina from around Wells's time; Ida's schoolhouse probably wasn't this nice.

Prospective white voters were asked easy questions, such as "Explain freedom of speech." Would-be black voters were asked difficult questions, such as "Explain the part of the Constitution that says 'all duties, imposts, and excises shall be uniform throughout the United States.'" Another trick was to switch polling places at the last second, so that black voters wouldn't know where to cast their ballot. Yet another was to hire thugs to stand around the voting places and intimidate the blacks into leaving. The result was that during the late 1800s fewer and fewer black people voted and the number of southern black politicians dwindled to practically zero.

Segregation became a way of life throughout the South during this time. The southern states passed numerous Jim Crow laws, as legislation segregating blacks and whites was called (named for a character in an old song-and-dance routine). Acts separating the races in schools and on trains were among the first Jim Crow laws. That was just the beginning, as blacks and whites became segregated by law or custom in all aspects of life.

Blacks and whites were forbidden to intermarry, and any southern minister who performed an interracial marriage risked being fined or jailed. The races were segregated in hospitals, orphanages, and insane asylums, and were even kept apart in poorhouses, so that hungry and homeless white people wouldn't have to associate with poor blacks. If separate buildings weren't available, black and white people were quartered in separate wings or floors of the same building. Rarely were the black facilities as well equipped as the white ones.

Separate public bathrooms, drinking fountains, and building entrances were constructed for whites and blacks throughout the South. Black children were taught at an early age to distinguish the signs WHITES ONLY and COLORED from one another, for it meant trouble if they were caught using a bathroom or drinking fountain for white people. Blacks weren't allowed to serve on juries, and when testifying in court, they had to swear on a separate Bible that whites wouldn't touch. When whites approached on the sidewalk, black people were expected to step out of the way. Blacks weren't supposed to shake hands with white people, and were expected to say "Yes, ma'am" and "Yes, sir" if addressed by them. On the other hand, white southerners referred to black people by their first names or simply by the term "nigger."

Not only was it forbidden for whites and blacks to dance or socialize together, they couldn't play baseball or checkers with one another. North Carolina and Florida even passed laws specifying that textbooks used by black and white children couldn't be stored together! When no longer able to care for themselves, white and black southerners entered segregated old-age homes. Separation of the races did not end there, for after southerners died, they were laid to rest in segregated cemeteries.

The police and white mobs enforced these laws and customs. Black people who entered "Whites Only" establishments might be jailed and fined. Blacks attempting to vote might be beaten. A black man caught dancing with a white girl risked a severe beating. A black man who fought with a white man, or who had sexual relations with a white woman, was liable to be lynched. A mob would gather and the victim would be seized and killed, generally by hanging, without benefit of a trial. The lynchers almost always escaped punishment; in fact, they were often praised by legal authorities and local newspapers for "keeping the niggers in line," as white southerners phrased it.

Ida had been teaching a short while when Grandmother Peggy suffered a stroke, which paralyzed her. She was taken away by relatives and spent her last years on a family farm. Ida then found an old friend of her mother's to stay with her brothers and sisters while she continued to teach at her country school. Her monthly salary of twenty-five dollars enabled Ida to meet her family's needs.

After about two years of this grueling schedule, however, Ida was worn out. Two of her aunts came to her rescue. Aunt Belle volunteered to care for Eugenia and to put James and George to work on her farm. Aunt Fannie invited Ida, Annie, and Lily to move into her Memphis home. The Wells children packed their belongings, left their childhood home in Holly Springs, and moved in with their two aunts.

Once in Memphis, Ida obtained a teaching position in Woodstock, Tennessee, ten miles north of the city. Instead of traveling by mule, she now went to work by train. During the summer she took teachers' training courses at LeMoyne Institute in Memphis and at Fisk University in Nashville, for she hoped to pass the more difficult examination to become a city schoolteacher.

In 1881 Tennessee passed its first Jim Crow law, specifying that black and white train passengers ride in separate cars. Ida defied this law and continued to ride to and from her school in what was called the Ladies' Coach. On May 4, 1884, Ida was reading a book in the Ladies' Coach en route to school when the conductor ordered her to move to the "Colored" train car. She refused, insisting on her right to stay where she was.

The conductor tried to drag Ida from her seat, but as he grabbed her, she bit his hand and he let go. The angry conductor wasn't finished. When the train stopped at a station, he fetched the stationmaster and the baggage man for assistance. A crowd of white people piled into the Ladies' Coach to watch the spectacle of three men trying to eject the young black woman. Several of them stood on the seats and cheered the white men on. Bracing her feet against the seat in front of her, the schoolteacher waged a valiant fight, but the men finally succeeded in pulling her away. Rather than go into the "Colored" car, Ida got off the train. Her clothes had been torn, and she had been bruised in several places.

Twenty-one-year-old Ida B. Wells decided to take on the powerful Chesapeake & Ohio Railroad. She hired the only black lawyer in Memphis and sued the railroad for discriminatory practices. The case was important, for if she won, it might slow the spread of the Jim Crow laws in the South. But while the case was pending, Ida discovered that her lawyer had been "bought off by the road," as she wrote in her autobiography. In other words, the railroad had bribed him to lose the case on purpose. Ida was especially hurt because she had expected a member of her race to take a personal interest in her case. Still, she refused to give up. She hired James M. Greer, a white lawyer who had been a Union officer during the Civil War, to represent her. Greer did an outstanding job, and on Christmas Eve, 1884, the circuit court ruled that the "plaintiff [Wells] was wrongfully ejected from the defendant's [the

An African American being expelled from a railroad car in Philadelphia, as drawn for a journal in England in 1856

railroad's] car." The judge concluded his ruling by ordering that the railroad pay Ida B. Wells five hundred dollars in damages.

On December 25, 1884, the *Memphis Appeal-Avalanche* ran an article about the decision. Ida must have felt a sense of satisfaction on that Christmas Day as she saw the headline: A DARKY DAMSEL OBTAINS A VERDICT FOR DAMAGES AGAINST THE CHESAPEAKE & OHIO RAILROAD—VERDICT FOR $500. At the age of twenty-two she had defeated a mighty railroad, struck a blow at Tennessee's first Jim Crow law, and found at least one white lawyer and one white judge who were interested in fair play. Ida had also taken the first step in what would become her lifelong crusade for justice.

Memphis during the 1890s

The Princess of the Press

I N THE FALL OF 1884, a few weeks before the circuit court ruled that the railroad should pay her five hundred dollars, Ida B. Wells passed the test to become a schoolteacher in Memphis. She was assigned to a first-grade class at the city's all-black Saffarans School. At about that time Aunt Fannie moved west to California, taking Annie and Lily as well as her own three children with her. With Eugenia, James, and George living on Aunt Belle's farm, Ida was left on her own in Memphis.

Her life changed dramatically. Although her salary rose to sixty dollars a month, teaching in the city was even more difficult than it had been out in the country. Her class averaged about seventy pupils— about three times the number of students a first-grade teacher would expect to have today. Living in the city was also very expensive. Ida sent part of her salary to her aunts to help them raise her sisters and brothers, leaving her without enough money for her own needs. Since she couldn't afford a house or apartment, Ida moved every few months from one dilapidated rooming house to another.

Still, Ida felt exhilarated to be on her own, as she revealed in the diary that she began in 1885. Despite the demands of teaching, she enjoyed an active social life. She made many friends, with whom she attended concerts and plays. Several male admirers called on her regularly. Ida and her gentleman friends played checkers and Parcheesi and went

Ida's class in Memphis may have looked somewhat like this.

strolling through town. At one point Ida counted five young men who were in love with her, but she didn't find any of them interesting enough to marry.

With other teacher friends she joined the Lyceum, a literary club that met Friday evenings at a Memphis church. Its members performed music and skits and recited their own poems and essays. Surprised to find that she had dramatic talent, Ida considered becoming an actress. At the time, however, there were few opportunities for black actors. For example, Ira Aldridge, a great Shakespearean actor of the 1800s, fled to Europe because of the prejudice and lack of opportunity he encountered in the United States.

The Lyceum had its own newspaper, the *Evening Star,* which contained local news items and a gossip column called "They Say." Each Friday night the editor read the newspaper aloud for the entertainment of club members. When the *Evening Star*'s editor moved to Washington, D.C., Ida was elected to replace him. She immensely enjoyed writing the newspaper and reading it aloud. The *Evening Star* became so popular in Memphis's black community that people who weren't members of the Lyceum began to pack the church on Friday nights to hear her read it.

One Friday night R. N. Countee, a Baptist minister in Memphis who published a black church weekly called the *Living Way,* came to hear Ida read the *Evening Star.* Reverend Countee was greatly impressed by her ability and asked her to write a weekly column for his newspaper. He couldn't pay her, he explained, but the *Living Way* would offer a wider readership and allow her to write more thought-provoking articles than did the Lyceum newsletter.

Ida accepted Reverend Countee's offer and began writing a column for the *Living Way* under the pen name "Iola." According to her granddaughter, Alfreda Duster Ferrell, when Ida was about eighteen years old she had seen her name on a document. But *Ida* had been written so hurriedly that the circle and stem of the *d* looked like two letters—*ol.* As a result her name looked like *Iola,* not *Ida.* She took a fancy to the name Iola and adopted it when she started her journalistic career.

In the 1880s few women went into journalism, and black female journalists were so rare that only about fifteen of them wrote for the nation's approximately two hundred black newspapers. Most female journalists of the time—black and white—wrote on subjects that were considered women's topics, which included book reviews, school news, and articles about marriage and children. For a black woman to write about racial issues was virtually unheard of, but that was what Iola did from the start.

Iola was as likely to criticize black people as white people. In one of her first articles, "Functions of Leadership," published in the *Living Way* on September 12, 1885, she complained about prominent blacks who did nothing "to alleviate the poverty and misery" of their people. In a later article, "Iola on Discrimination," she criticized whites for bigotry against blacks, and black people for not doing more to fight segregation.

Reverend Countee distributed the *Living Way* to black newspapers

"Iola" on Discrimination.

From the American Baptist.

We howl about the discrimination exercised by other races, unmindful that we are guilty of the same thing. The spirit that keeps Negroes out of the colleges and places him by himself, is the same that drives him in the smoking car; the spirit that makes colored men run excursions with "a separate car for our white friends," etc., provides separate seats for them when they visit our concerts, exhibitions, etc., is the same that sends the Negro to theatre and church galleries and second class waiting rooms; the feeling that prompts colored barbers, hotel keepers and the like to refuse accommodation to their own color is the momentum that sends a Negro right about when he presents himself at any similar first-class establishment run by white men; the shortsightedness that insists on separate Knights of Labor Assemblies for colored men, is the same power that forces them into separate Masonic and Odd Fellow lodges. Consciously and unconsciously we do as much to widen the breach already existing and to keep prejudice alive as the other race. There was not a separate school in the State of California until the colored people asked for it. To say we wish to be to ourselves is a tacit acknowledgement of the inferiority that they take for granted anyway. The ignorant man who is so shortsighted has some excuse, but the man or men who deliberately yield or barter the birthright of the race for money, position, self-aggrandizement in any form, deserve and will receive the contumely of a race made wise by experience.   IOLA.

Memphis, Tenn., Dec. 28, 1886.

around the country. A number of them, including the *Little Rock (Arkansas) Sun* and the *Washington (D.C.) Bee,* reprinted Iola's articles. Several other journals asked her to write articles for them, including the *New York Freeman,* a major newspaper edited by T. Thomas Fortune. Most of the newspapers paid her with free copies, but one day Reverend William J. Simmons, editor of the *American Baptist,* came to Memphis from Kentucky to see her. Reverend Simmons said that he wanted to meet "the brilliant Iola," and he offered her one dollar a week to write for the *American Baptist*. Wells later recalled in her autobiography: "It was the first time anyone had offered to pay me for the work I had enjoyed doing. I had never dreamed of receiving any pay, for I had been too happy over the thought that the papers were giving me space."

Iola became famous among black newspaper readers. T. Thomas Fortune wrote: "She has plenty of nerve, she is as smart as a steel trap, and she has no sympathy with humbug." The public grew curious about what Iola looked like, so several newspapers published her picture, then argued over whether or not she was attractive. The *Cleveland Gazette* actually criticized her for "trying to be pretty as well as smart," advising her to "remember that beauty and genius are not always companions."

Ida was flattered by all the attention, and by her nickname among black readers: the Princess of the Press. Yet she often felt restless and dissatisfied with her life. She was a good teacher, but she found the job

"The Princess of the Press"; from an 1891 book, The Afro-American Press and Its Editors, *by I. Garland Penn*

too frustrating to make it her life's work. Most of her female friends were married or about to be. Although women were expected to be wives by the age of twenty-one or twenty-two, Ida in her mid-twenties still had no interest in marriage. She loved newspaper work, which "gave me an outlet through which to express the real 'me,'" but she couldn't live on the one dollar a week Reverend Simmons paid her.

In June of 1886, about the time school closed for the summer, Ida received a letter postmarked California. Aunt Fannie wanted Ida to apply for a teaching position in Visalia, the town where Fannie had settled with her own children and Ida's sisters Annie and Lily. Ida had mixed feelings about her aunt's suggestion. She wanted to stay in Memphis, where she had friends, cultural opportunities, and her newspaper work; she had no desire to move to a dusty town in central California that she could barely find on the map. Yet she felt a debt of gratitude to Aunt Fannie, who said she needed her help in raising Annie and Lily. Ida wrote back saying that she would visit Visalia for the summer but probably wouldn't settle there. She resolved that if Aunt Fannie could no longer raise Annie and Lily, she would bring them back to Memphis with her.

Reduced-rate group tours known as excursions were popular in the late 1800s. Ida learned about a National Educational Association excursion from Memphis to Topeka, Kansas, where there was to be a teachers' convention. She and several teacher friends departed from Memphis by train on July 4. After attending the conference, Ida signed up for an excursion to California, arriving in Visalia on August 1 after a journey of more than two thousand miles from Memphis.

Ida had a happy reunion with her sisters, aunt, and three cousins. Now thirteen and ten years old, Annie and Lily were growing up, but Ida was shocked to find that raising five children had transformed Aunt Fannie into a careworn old woman. When her aunt asked her to remain in Visalia to help with the children, Ida agreed. "I will not run and leave her alone," she wrote in her diary. She sold her return train ticket and

Robert Reed Church

accepted the teaching position offered by Visalia's school superintendent.

No sooner had Ida agreed to live in Visalia for a year than she regretted not returning to Memphis with her sisters. She found the town dull, and disappointing in another way. Although the West bragged about its "pioneer spirit," where everyone was supposed to be equal, Ida found that in some respects California was as segregated as Tennessee. For example, schools were segregated. While Visalia's white students attended a large, well-kept school, Ida was to teach the town's eighteen black students in a one-room shack.

Ida began to worry about what she would do if she hated her teaching job. She couldn't just run off without her sisters, and yet she didn't have enough money to take them back with her to Tennessee. A few weeks before the start of the school year, she decided to seek help from Robert Reed Church, the wealthy black Memphis man who had been shot by police during the 1866 race riot. Church was known for his good deeds. Following the 1878 yellow fever epidemic, Memphis lost so much of its population and was so deeply in debt that Tennessee's legislature took away its city charter. Church bought the first municipal bonds that helped Memphis regain its city charter. Ida wrote Church a letter, requesting a loan of one hundred fifty dollars in case she wanted to take her sisters to Memphis. He was the only black person she knew who could lend her that much money and wait for her to repay it, she explained.

Mail between California and Tennessee was slow. When school opened in Visalia in early September, Ida had not heard from Mr. Church. As she had feared, she found teaching in Visalia oppressive. Then, on the second day of school, in the middle of class, a telegram was delivered to her. She opened it and was surprised to read: "You were elected to teach in the Kansas City schools last night. Wire when to expect you."

Some people she had met at the education convention had arranged for her to teach in Kansas City, Missouri. Two days later she received a letter from Mr. Church. Along with a check for one hundred fifty dollars, he enclosed an explanation that her old teaching job in Memphis was waiting for her if she wanted it.

Ida quickly made up her mind. After just four days of teaching in Visalia, she sent a telegram accepting the offer from Kansas City, saying that she was "leaving tonight." She resigned from the Visalia school, thanked Aunt Fannie for all she had done, and told her sisters to pack. But Aunt Fannie didn't want Annie and Lily to leave her, Ida discovered. As her aunt pleaded with her three nieces to stay, Ida realized that Fannie was lonely and craved their companionship. Yet Ida also knew that her life would be miserable if she remained in Visalia. Ida and her aunt agreed that Annie, who couldn't bear to leave her cousins, could stay in Visalia. Ida and Lily then said good-bye to their relatives and took the train east.

The new teacher and her ten-year-old sister arrived in Kansas City the day after school had begun. Black leaders were excited to have the famous Iola in their community. In addition to her teaching duties Wells was asked to write articles for the *Gate City Press,* a popular black newspaper in Kansas City. But when she went to her school and took over the fourth-grade class, she found herself in an uncomfortable position. She had replaced a local teacher who was well liked, and the staff resented her for it.

At the end of the first day Ida entered the principal's office and resigned, explaining that she hadn't come to Kansas City to take anyone's job or hurt anyone's feelings. She and Lily boarded the train for Memphis that same night and arrived just in time for the start of the new school year. Thus, in September 1886, Ida B. Wells had the unusual experience of teaching in three states within two weeks—California, Missouri, and Tennessee.

The 1886–87 school year proved to be a miserable one for Ida. She was assigned a rowdy class (apparently fourth grade) of about seventy pupils, who drained her energy. What with repaying the one hundred fifty dollars to Mr. Church and sending money to California to help her aunt pay for Annie's expenses, Ida had little money remaining. She also suffered family problems. Lily didn't get along with the landlady of the rooming house where they were staying, and she often disobeyed Ida, reminding her that she was her sister, not her mother. Ida became frustrated with her little sister. As she confided in her diary: "Had to whip Lily severely this morning. I earnestly pray such may never happen again." On March 1, 1887, Grandmother Peggy died. Ida's teenaged brothers, James and George, had left Aunt Belle's farm and become involved with bad company in the Memphis area, and Ida often had to bail them out of trouble when they got drunk and gambled.

Moreover, Ida remained uncertain about her own future. Her dream to become a full-time journalist seemed hopeless. On days when her students misbehaved more than usual, she thought of moving out to the country with her family and starting a chicken farm. But soon she wondered how she had ever considered such an idea. On March 20, 1887, she confessed to her diary: "I am not happy & nothing seems to make me so. I wonder what kind of a creature I will eventually become?"

A few days later Ida suffered a terrible blow. She had not received the five hundred dollars that the circuit court had ordered the Chesapeake & Ohio Railroad to pay her for its discriminatory practices against black people. Instead, the C&O's lawyer had visited her to offer her several hundred dollars to "compromise the case," as she called it in her autobiography. The lawyer apparently threatened to appeal the case to Tennessee's Supreme Court unless Wells backed down in some way. Aware of her influence among black readers, the railroad may have wanted her to write an article saying that segregation on trains wasn't so bad. Wells was offended by the railroad's offer and angrily refused it. Just twenty-four years old and highly idealistic, she wholeheartedly believed that if she did what was right, justice would prevail.

As threatened, the railroad took the case to Tennessee's highest court, which rendered its decision on April 5, 1887, nearly two and a half years after the circuit court's ruling. The State Supreme Court ruled in favor of the C&O, saying that Wells had intended to "harass" the railroad by her lawsuit and ordering her to pay more than two hundred dollars in court costs. Wells was crushed by the verdict. The justices had ignored the evidence and had made their decision according to "personal prejudices" against black people, Ida's lawyer sadly told her. Upon learning of the decision, Ida wrote in her diary:

> I felt so disappointed, because I had hoped such great things from my suit for my people generally. I have firmly believed all along that the law was on our side and would, when we appealed to it, give us justice. I feel shorn of that belief and utterly discouraged, and just now if it were possible would gather my race in my arms and fly far away with them. O God is there no redress, no peace, no justice in this land for us? Thou hast always fought the battles of the weak &

oppressed. Come to my aid at this moment & teach me what to do, for I am sorely, bitterly disappointed. Show us the way.

This experience was a turning point in Wells's life, for although it disillusioned her, it also sparked a rage against injustice that would always

Page from Ida's diary, in which she wrote, "I felt so disappointed . . ." on April 11, 1887

remain with her. And while the decision broke her heart, it toughened her spirit.

★

Over the next few years Wells continued to write for such newspapers as T. Thomas Fortune's *New York Age* (formerly the *New York Freeman*), the *Detroit Plaindealer,* the *Indianapolis World,* the *Chattanooga Justice,* and the *Gate City Press* of Kansas City. She became so well known for her articles about racial discrimination that when she attended the Afro-American Press Convention in Washington, D.C., in 1889, she was unanimously elected convention secretary. She met several renowned black leaders at the convention, including Frederick Douglass, a former slave who had become the nineteenth century's most famous spokesman for the rights of African Americans. Douglass liked and admired the Princess of the Press, who, about forty-five years his junior, was young enough to be his granddaughter.

Shortly after the convention, Wells was invited to write articles for the *Free Speech and Headlight,* a black newspaper in Memphis with a large circulation and an interesting history. Reverend Taylor Nightingale, a Baptist preacher with the largest black congregation in Tennessee, had operated a Memphis newspaper called the *Free Speech.* Just across the Mississippi River in Marion, Arkansas, a journalist named J. L. Fleming had published a black newspaper called the *Marion Headlight.* White bigots had driven Fleming out of Marion in 1888. Crossing the river into Memphis, Fleming had joined forces with Reverend Nightingale to combine their papers as the *Free Speech and Headlight.*

Recognizing the offer as a great opportunity, Wells agreed to write for Reverend Nightingale and Mr. Fleming's paper under one condition: She was to become a part owner and the editor. This suited the two men, who were more interested in advertisements, subscriptions, and other business matters than in actually producing the newspaper. In the summer of 1889 Wells scraped together the money and bought a one-third interest in the *Free Speech and Headlight,* becoming one of the country's few black female newspaper owners and editors.

The new editor thought the paper's name was too long, so one of her first changes was to rename it simply the *Free Speech.* Wells's fiery style terrified Mr. Fleming, who had already been run out of one town, and disturbed Reverend Nightingale, who had convinced many white and black businessmen to advertise in the paper. Wells criticized injustice wherever she saw it, not caring who didn't like it. For example, the *Free Speech* harshly condemned Isaiah Montgomery, the only black member of a convention that created a new constitution for Mississippi in 1890. White delegates to the convention wanted to deprive black Mississippians of the vote by adding a Constitution test to the voting laws. Wells ripped into Montgomery for going along with his white colleagues rather than standing up for what was right and fighting the proposal.

In 1891 Wells wrote an article about the Memphis schools, charging that white authorities were cheating black children out of a decent education. At the time, the newspaper was barely breaking even financially, and Wells still depended upon her teaching job for her livelihood. Just before the paper went to press, she showed Reverend Nightingale the article and asked him to sign his name to it, for she suspected that the school authorities would fire her if her name were on the piece.

Reverend Nightingale read the article, then shook his head. The editorial was too strongly worded, he felt, and would bring the wrath of the white community down upon him. Wells knew the article was too important to withdraw or tone down, so she placed her name on it and "let it ride."

The article threw Memphis into an uproar. The board of education, other white citizens, and even some blacks were angered by her criticisms of the schools for black children. As a result, after more than ten years as a teacher, Ida B. Wells was fired by the Memphis schools. Without exactly planning it, the Princess of the Press had become a full-time journalist.

The Lynching That Changed Ida's Life

SOON AFTER THE ARTICLE about the Memphis schools appeared, Reverend Nightingale retired from the *Free Speech,* leaving Ida B. Wells and J. L. Fleming to run the paper. Wells believed that she might be able to earn a living from the *Free Speech* if she could make it more interesting and boost its circulation. Using a press pass, which allowed her to ride trains without paying, she began visiting Mississippi River towns in Tennessee, Arkansas, and Mississippi. Wherever black people met in large numbers in a church or hall, she tried to be there to gather news and sell subscriptions.

At Greenville, Mississippi, she attended a convention of black lawyers, all of whom signed up for *Free Speech* subscriptions. At Water Valley, Mississippi, not far from her birthplace of Holly Springs, she spoke to a statewide meeting of black Masons, many of whom had known her father. "When I came out of that meeting," she recalled in her autobiography, "I was weighted down with silver dollars and had to go straight to the bank." She also depended upon stringers—people not on the newspaper staff who provided her with information for articles. One of them was Thomas Moss, a letter carrier who delivered mail to the *Free Speech* office on Hernando Street. Whatever news Tommie had heard he shared with Wells so that she could scoop the other papers. Ida became so friendly with Tommie Moss and his wife, Betty, that they named her godmother of their daughter, Maurine.

In the 1890s "news butchers" sold newspapers and magazines to passengers on trains. Soon the *Free Speech* was in demand all along the railroad line that ran along the Mississippi River. Many of the passengers who purchased the *Free Speech* could not read, and planned to have someone read the paper aloud to them. A few news butchers took advantage of this situation by substituting copies of newspapers that weren't selling well to customers who had paid for the *Free Speech*. Wells solved this problem by switching to pink newsprint for the *Free Speech,* so that people unable to read could ask for the pink paper. Within about nine months she had increased the *Free Speech*'s circulation from fifteen hundred to four thousand and was earning nearly the salary that she had made as a teacher.

The twenty-nine-year-old editor was drumming up subscriptions in Natchez, Mississippi, in March 1892, when she received distressing news. To help with the payments for a little house in Memphis that he and Betty had bought, Tommie Moss had begun a second job. With two partners he had opened the People's Grocery in a neighborhood that was called the Curve because of the sharp turn the streetcar line made at that point. His partners, Calvin McDowell and Will Stewart, worked in the grocery during the day, while Tommie went there on Sundays and at night after he had completed his mail route.

Nearly everyone who knew Tommie Moss and his partners respected them for their ambition and hard work. An exception was a white man named Barrett, who operated a grocery store across the street from the People's Grocery. Although the Curve was a predominantly black neighborhood, Barrett had enjoyed a monopoly among the area's shoppers until the rival store opened. As he lost customers, Barrett looked for a way to eliminate his competitors.

One day some boys, both black and white, got into a fight over a game of marbles near the People's Grocery. Unfortunately, the fight spread to the boys' fathers. Barrett claimed that the People's Grocery had caused a riot in the neighborhood and tried to have the store's

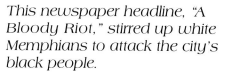

A BLOODY RIOT.

Deputies Shot By Negroes.

A Horrible Affair at the Curve Late Last Night.

A Nest of Outlaws Disturbed and Shotguns Fired at Officers.

Three of Them Very Seriously Hurt By the Bullets.

Deputy Sheriffs Cole, Harold and Yerger the Suffering Victims.

Thirteen of the Black and Bloody-Handed Miscreants Arrested.

The Condition of Deputy Sheriff Cole Very Serious---The Others Will Recover--- A Large Lot of Weapons Captured. The Dive Long Known as a Disturbance Breeder---A Full Account of the Affair.

Three deputy sheriffs shot.

One of them will die, and another is very badly hurt.

Thirteen negroes are immured in cells at the station-house.

A force of policemen and deputy sheriffs are searching for others who were engaged in the rencontre.

crowd of 20 or 30 shotguns, rifles and four negro prisoners, in mud, with irons quaking with terror, mutterings and sug and lamp-posts, and right proposition to ing low right them, that Harold, Cole an are popular with the they were as indign they did their duty under guard.

A posse they poss church, where some supposed to have b There was no one search of a number of n the arrest of four them Armour Harris brought on the who was one of the crow the shooting occurred found. The mother gingers and abused t invading her house.

As the posse mare handcuffed to a big y caught on the high in his pocket, the vi "March on like a Lawd's wid you an' Armour didn't need cepted the fact of h fortitude.

A posse of four th of Hugh Williams, w been the ringleader who handled one of t such havoc in the Williams is only 26 perate character. Williams, who was of W. H. Person. Williams residence is house, on College ave the old man up and s it was midnight, b home. Another youn the house, however, of on suspicion, as account of himself.

Several other hou then the Appeal-Av to town. At 3 o'cloc

This newspaper headline, "A Bloody Riot," stirred up white Memphians to attack the city's black people.

owners arrested. When that failed, he threatened to "clean out the whole store." Word spread that on Saturday night, March 5, 1892, Barrett was going to bring a white mob to destroy the business that Thomas Moss, Calvin McDowell, and Will Stewart had worked so hard to build.

Moss and his partners consulted a lawyer and were told that because the Curve was beyond the Memphis city limits, they could not obtain protection from the Memphis police. Therefore they had every right to defend themselves if attacked. On Saturday night the grocers stationed several armed men in the back of the store to defend their lives and property.

Barrett concocted a sneaky plan. In areas of a county not patrolled by city police, sheriffs maintained law and order. Barrett told the sheriff of Shelby County, in which Memphis is located, that criminals were hiding in the People's Grocery. Had the sheriff really believed that, he would have investigated the situation himself. Instead, he deputized several men, meaning that he made ordinary citizens temporary law officers. At eleven o'clock on Saturday night, Barrett, the deputies, and several other white men looking for trouble broke into the People's Grocery through the back door. Thinking—probably correctly—that they were about to be attacked, the grocery guards fired their guns. Three of the intruders were wounded, and the rest fled.

Although they had been wearing civilian clothes, hadn't identified themselves, and had broken into the store like thieves, the three wounded men turned out to be among the so-called deputies. With Barrett's help, by Sunday morning the white newspapers as well as Memphis authorities had completely distorted the facts. Moss, McDowell, and Stewart, who had, in fact, been model citizens, were characterized as "Negro desperadoes." A newspaper referred to their store as "a resort of thieves and thugs" and predicted that the store owners would be dealt with extremely harshly if any of the wounded "law officers" should die.

Word of the shootings spread through Memphis, and on Sunday morning the police poured into the Curve. They went from house to house, arresting dozens of black people on suspicion of being involved in the shootings. Certain that they had done nothing wrong and that they could prove their guards had fired in self-defense, Moss, McDowell, and Stewart immediately surrendered to authorities and were locked in jail.

All day Sunday groups of white ruffians, many of them drunk, stood on street corners near the jail threatening to "lynch the niggers." Memphis's black community feared that the three men would be dragged from the jail and murdered. In those times states had militia units, similar to today's National Guard, that mobilized in emergencies. A black militia unit called the Tennessee Rifles gathered around the Memphis jail to guard the storekeepers. All through Sunday and Monday nights the Tennessee Rifles stood watch. On Tuesday the newspapers announced that the three wounded deputies were recovering. Thinking that the prisoners would be safe, the Tennessee Rifles withdrew.

The mob decided that the fact that the three black storekeepers had stood up for their rights was sufficient reason to lynch them. On Tuesday night, while Thomas Moss, Calvin McDowell, and Will Stewart slept in their cells, a group of men either broke into the jail or were let

Article describing the death of the three storekeepers; Calvin McDowell (left) and Thomas Moss are pictured, as is the murder scene, at bottom.

in by authorities. They were probably let in, for none of the jail guards attempted to protect the prisoners. The mob pulled the storekeepers from their cells and shoved them onto a railroad engine on the tracks behind the jail. The three men were taken a mile north of the Memphis city limits, where they were lined up and asked if they had anything to say before they died.

Thomas Moss begged for his life for the sake of his wife, daughter, and unborn baby. When he realized that it was hopeless, he said, "Tell my people to go West. There is no justice for them here." Seconds later the mob opened fire from close range. Apparently McDowell attempted to grab one of the attackers' guns, for the fingers on his right hand were shot off. Because he tried to fight back, McDowell also had his eyes gouged out while he was being shot to pieces. Within minutes all three men were dead.

But the mob wasn't finished. The murderers were worried that the black people of Memphis might seek revenge for the killings. The Shelby County sheriff went to the judge of the criminal court, who told him, "Take a hundred men, go out to the Curve at once, and shoot down on sight any Negro who appears to be making trouble."

The sheriff led the mob out to the Curve, but they didn't find anyone to shoot. News of the murder of the storekeepers had spread, and the black residents were all indoors, determined to avoid trouble. The mob vented its frustration by shooting off their guns in the neighborhood and breaking into the empty People's Grocery. They ate and drank all they could, stole the rest of the stock, and wrecked the store.

Upon learning of the murder of her friend and his partners, Ida B. Wells returned home from Natchez. She did what she could to comfort Betty Moss and her daughter, Maurine. The enraged newspaper editor vowed that the *Free Speech* would battle the lynchers and the people who "looked the other way," and that she wouldn't rest until the world knew the truth about the matter. She picked up her pen and wrote an editorial that appeared in her newspaper a few days after the murders:

The city of Memphis has demonstrated that neither character nor standing avails the Negro if he dares to protect himself against the white man or become his rival. There is nothing we can do about the lynching now, as we are outnumbered and without arms. The white mob could help itself to ammunition, but the order was rigidly enforced against the selling of guns to Negroes. There is therefore only one thing left that we can do: Save our money and leave a town which will neither protect our lives and property, nor give us a fair trial in the courts, but takes us out and murders us in cold blood when accused by white persons.

Wells's advice that black people should "leave a town which murders us in cold blood" and Thomas Moss's dying plea to "tell my people to go West" were repeated over and over by the city's black residents, hundreds of whom packed up and fled Memphis. Several ministers, including R. N. Countee, publisher of the *Living Way,* convinced most of their congregations to leave the city. Some black Memphians crossed the Mississippi River and settled in Arkansas. Others left the South entirely and moved to such places as California and Kansas. Betty Moss remained in Memphis until the birth of her son, whom she named Thomas Moss Jr. She then abandoned the city where her husband had been murdered and moved with Tommie Jr. and Maurine to Indiana.

People who could not afford to leave Memphis by train walked or traveled in wagons, like the pioneers of a generation or two earlier. Wells reported that a huge crowd gathered to watch a group of three hundred black people depart in their wagons. When the time came for the group to leave, an old man in one of the wagons couldn't catch his dog. The old man yelled out to the animal, "Come on here. What you want to stay back there for? Want the white folks to lynch you, too?"

Many black people who remained in Memphis refused to work for white families or shop at white businesses anymore. Among the busi-

Picture taken in an unknown location after Ida and the Moss family moved away from Memphis; Ida (left) with Maurine, Betty, and Tommie Moss Jr.

nesses that suffered was the City Railway Company, which ran the Memphis streetcars. One day the company's superintendent and treasurer visited the *Free Speech* office and asked Wells to advise black people to ride the streetcars again.

"The streetcar company had nothing to do with the lynching," said one of the men.

"We have learned that every white man of any standing in town knew of the plan and consented to the lynching of our boys," Wells responded. "Did you know Tom Moss, the letter carrier? A finer man than he never walked the streets of Memphis. He was well liked, a favorite with everybody, yet he was murdered because he defended his property from attack. The colored people feel that every white man in Memphis who consented to his death is as guilty as those who fired the guns which took his life."

"Why don't the colored people find the guilty ones?" asked one of the men.

"As if they could!" she answered. "There is strong belief among us that the criminal court judge himself was one of the lynchers."

After the men left her office, Wells wrote up the conversation and published it in the next issue of the *Free Speech,* along with her advice that black people should maintain their boycott of white businesses.

Within two months, six thousand of Memphis's thirty thousand blacks had moved away, and still the exodus continued. In the early 1890s parts of Oklahoma were opened to settlement. Fearing that this would prompt more black Memphians to depart, the same newspapers that had inflamed the lynchers claimed that only harsh weather, starvation, and hostile Indians awaited settlers in Oklahoma. For example, the March 23, 1892, *Memphis Appeal-Avalanche* warned, "The Negroes of this section who are preparing to go to Oklahoma should bear in mind the fact that the [bad] weather which has marked the past few days in the vicinity of Memphis is not an unusual thing in that country."

Wells decided to visit Oklahoma and learn the truth for herself. In the spring of 1892 she took the train to Kansas City, and from there traveled into Oklahoma. She spent three weeks visiting Guthrie, Oklahoma City, and other towns in Oklahoma. Wells liked what she saw, and she wrote letters back to the *Free Speech* describing Oklahoma as a land of opportunity. Hundreds of black Memphians were soon heading to Oklahoma, in many cases walking the five hundred miles.

Meanwhile, Wells had decided to learn more about lynchings in the

South, thus becoming one of the world's first investigative reporters, as we call them today. One frightening fact she uncovered was that Memphis had nearly suffered a far bloodier massacre than the killing of the three storekeepers. A prominent white man in Memphis revealed, "You got off light. We first intended to kill every one of those thirty-one niggers in jail, but concluded to let all go but the leaders."

The murders of the three Memphis storekeepers were part of a larger problem, Wells learned. In her research she discovered that the word *lynching* dated from the 1700s, when the American colonies were

LEFT: *Sign in Virginia marking the spot where Charles Lynch whipped British sympathizers.* RIGHT: *One of the first photographs of a lynching: John Heith, a white man, was lynched in Arizona on February 22, 1884.*

rebelling against England. Some colonists who sided with England were whipped and driven from their homes by mobs of American patriots. These beatings were called lynchings for Virginian Charles Lynch, who authorized attacks against British sympathizers.

After independence, lynching continued, but changed. Instead of British sympathizers, those attacked by lynchers were people accused of such crimes as murder, rape, and arson, and they were often killed, not just beaten. By the mid-1800s "lynching" meant the murder of a person by a mob, usually by hanging.

The nation's founders felt so strongly about the right to a fair trial that they guaranteed it in the Bill of Rights, ten amendments to the Constitution that specify the basic liberties of all citizens. The Fifth Amendment states that no person shall "be deprived of life, liberty, or property, without due process of law." The Sixth Amendment states that "In all criminal prosecutions, the accused shall enjoy the right to a speedy and public trial" as well as the right "to be informed of the nature and cause of the accusation; to be confronted with the witnesses against him . . . and to have the assistance of counsel for his defense." Lynching victims were deprived of all these rights, which were considered fundamental American liberties by the Founding Fathers of this country.

Despite breaking the law, lynchers were rarely punished, for the mobs were generally large and often included community leaders. When they bothered to offer an explanation, lynchers made feeble excuses as to why they had taken the law into their own hands. The accused was obviously guilty, lynchers usually insisted, so why waste time and money on a trial? In rape cases the lynchers often claimed that they were saving the rape victims the embarrassment of having to testify in court.

At first, most lynching victims had been white. But by the 1880s, when lynching statistics were first kept, roughly half of the one hundred sixty people reported killed by mobs in a typical year were black.

The turning point was 1890, when eighty-five of the ninety-six people lynched were black. From then on, southern blacks were the main victims of lynch mobs.

The year 1892, when Ida B. Wells began her research, was the deadliest year for lynchings in U.S. history. Two hundred thirty people were known to have been murdered by mobs that year. The true figure could have been much higher, for many people who "disappeared" or died in suspicious "accidents" may have actually been lynched.

Besides gathering facts and figures, Wells investigated individual cases to learn about the people involved. She visited a town in Mississippi where a young black man had been lynched for allegedly raping a child. "The big burly brute was lynched because he had raped the seven-year-old daughter of the sheriff," claimed local newspapers. Wells discovered that the "child" was in fact over eighteen years old and hadn't been sexually attacked. She and the black youth had been lovers. The sheriff had found the couple together and concocted the rape story, inciting a mob to kill his daughter's boyfriend. The newspapers altered the facts to make it appear that the black youth had committed a terrible crime.

A house burned down in Monroe County, Alabama, and the bodies of a white family were found inside. Despite a lack of evidence, white neighbors claimed that black sharecroppers on the property had set the fire. Authorities arrested ten black people, four of whom were pulled from jail by a mob and killed. The lynchers weren't satisfied with just hanging Berrell Jones, Moses Johnson, and Jim and John Packer. They shot bullets into them and set them on fire as they dangled from the ropes. Ida B. Wells learned that the four lynched men had been on good terms with the white family that had died in the fire. She was convinced that the real arsonists had organized the lynching to hide their crime.

At Vicksburg, Mississippi, a murder was committed by a gang of burglars. A mob blamed two black men, John Adams and Smith Tooley, and hanged them on the courthouse grounds. Soon after, the burglars in the area were discovered to be white men who had blackened their faces. Wells believed that Adams and Tooley had been lynched by the very men involved in the robberies and murder.

Every lynching was an outrage against justice, but some, like the murder of the three Memphis storekeepers, were especially loathsome. Ebenezer Fowler, a respected black man, was shot to pieces by a white mob on the streets of Mayersville, Mississippi. His crime? He had written a note to a white woman. At Tullahoma, Tennessee, Will Lewis was hanged by a mob for having been "drunk and sassy to white folks."

Wells also encountered many "legal" lynchings—cases in which the accused received a trial in which the evidence wasn't considered fairly. A tragic example of this occurred in Columbia, South Carolina, after a white baby unexpectedly died. It was believed that the infant had been poisoned. Despite a lack of evidence, a thirteen-year-old black girl named Mildred Brown was found guilty of the crime and "legally" hanged.

Some of the facts Wells discovered shocked her. For one thing, southern newspapers encouraged lynching, sometimes announcing when and where a mob murder would occur. Not only local officials but also state governors encouraged lynchings. South Carolina's Governor Benjamin R. Tillman stood under a tree where eight black people had been lynched and boasted, "I would lead a mob to lynch a Negro who had raped a white woman." In Nashville, the capital of Tennessee, Governor John P. Buchanan refused to send out the militia to protect a black man, who was then dragged through the streets and stabbed and hanged by a mob.

A particularly disturbing fact came to light when Wells investigated the so-called rapes that incited so many lynchings. During the four years that white southerners had been away fighting the Civil War, leaving their wives and daughters alone with slaves, rape of white women by black men had been virtually unknown. Why would black men suddenly start raping white women a few years later? In most cases, Wells

Unidentified black man lynched in Florida, photographed by a traveling salesman; the fact that the victim is handcuffed is a clue that he was in the custody of law officers when murdered.

found, what had really happened was that a black man and a white woman fell in love and lived together, in violation of southern laws. Resentful white men accused the black man of rape and lynched him. Wells also learned that a few years earlier, J. C. Duke, editor of a black newspaper called the *Herald* of Montgomery, Alabama, had written that lynchings often occurred simply because some white and black people were attracted to each other. For stating this truth, J. C. Duke was driven out of Montgomery by a mob.

Two black men lynched in Indiana

Wells presented her findings in the *Free Speech*. Realizing that her articles placed her life in danger, she kept a pistol in her desk in her newspaper office. "I had bought a pistol the first thing after Tom Moss was lynched," she wrote in her autobiography, "because I expected some cowardly retaliation from the lynchers. I determined to sell my life as dearly as possible if attacked."

During a single week in May 1892, eight black people were lynched, five of whom had been accused of rape. Wells sat down with her gun by her side and wrote her angriest editorial yet:

> Eight Negroes lynched since the last issue of the *Free Speech* . . . five on the same old racket—the alarm about raping white women. The program of hanging, then shooting bullets into the lifeless bodies was carried out to the letter. Nobody in this section of the country believes the old threadbare lie that Negro men rape white women. If southern white men are not careful, they will overreach themselves and . . . a conclusion will be reached which will be very damaging to the moral reputation of their women.

The "conclusion" Wells meant was that black men and white women sometimes fell in love, and that what whites called rapes were generally love affairs between consenting adults. These were fighting words to southern white men, who in earlier times had fought duels over what they considered insults to the honor of their women. To southern white men the suggestion that their sisters and daughters could fall in love with black men was abhorrent, as was the implication that white women could in some cases prefer black men to themselves.

The *Free Speech,* which was a weekly publication, printed this editorial on Saturday, May 21, 1892. Fortunately for Wells, she had left on a trip east a few days before the editorial appeared. She went to Philadelphia to attend a convention of the African Methodist Episcopal (AME) Church, the oldest black religious denomination in the United States, and then visited New York City as the guest of T. Thomas Fortune, the editor of the *New York Age*.

Meanwhile, back in Memphis, Wells's editorial sent the city's white people into a frenzy of rage. The *Memphis Daily Commercial* called her a "black scoundrel" and asserted that the fact she was "allowed to live is evidence as to the wonderful patience of southern whites. But we have had enough of it." The *Memphis Scimitar* declared that "the wretch" who had written the *Free Speech* article should be "tied to a stake at the intersection of Main and Madison streets, branded in the forehead with a hot iron, and [tortured] with tailor's shears."

Stirred up by their newspapers, white Memphians held a "citizens' meeting," led by Edward Carmack, at the Cotton Exchange Building. Carmack, the *Daily Commercial* editor who had called Wells a "black scoundrel," was a notorious racist who once said that the prospect of black-white equality "fills the white man with loathing and disgust." Under his leadership the citizens' meeting spoke openly about lynching the perpetrators of the article and appointed a "committee" to deal with Ida B. Wells and J. L. Fleming, owners of the *Free Speech*.

Wells escaped the wrath of the committee only because she was out of town. Fleming might have been added to the list of lynching victims for 1892 had it not been for a white Memphis man who warned him to flee. The committee scoured Memphis, searching for Fleming, but he had slipped out of town just in time. Although Reverend Taylor Nightingale had retired from the *Free Speech* six months earlier, the mob seized him and beat him about the face. As a pistol was held to his head, Reverend Nightingale was told he would be permitted to live only if he signed a statement saying that the *Free Speech* editorial was a wicked slander on white women. With the gun to his head, Reverend Nightingale signed the statement.

The mob decided to make certain that the *Free Speech* wouldn't publish any more such editorials. They broke into Wells's office and destroyed the printing press and furniture. They also left a note threatening death to anyone who tried to publish the newspaper again. In case Ida B. Wells returned to Memphis, the committee assigned men to watch her home as well as the incoming trains. Reportedly their orders were to kill her on sight. Had Wells returned to Memphis, there might have been a tremendous riot, for the black men of the city were organizing to protect her.

Wells was unaware of all of this as she left the AME meeting in Philadelphia and took the train for New York City. T. Thomas Fortune met her at the station with a worried look on his face.

"Well," he said, "we've been a long time getting you to New York, but now that you are here, I am afraid you will have to stay."

T. Thomas Fortune

"I can't see why," Wells responded. "Will you please tell me what you are talking about?"

"Haven't you seen the morning paper?" he said, handing her a copy of the *New York Sun*.

Wells read how, twelve hundred miles away in Memphis, a mob had attacked the *Free Speech* office and threatened its owners' lives. The article went on to relate that one of those owners was Ida B. Wells, a former schoolteacher whose life had been spared only because she was traveling in the North.

Wells telegraphed friends in Memphis for news. They sent telegrams begging her not to return and informing her that guards posted by the committee were watching all incoming trains for any sign of her. Reports of what the mob planned to do if they captured her varied. One friend said that if she returned, she was to be hanged in front of the courthouse. Another said that she was to be beaten to death and her body dumped into the Mississippi River. Someone revealed to her where Mr. Fleming was hiding, so she was able to contact him and learn that he was unharmed. Despite having been driven out of both Arkansas and Tennessee, Fleming continued in the newspaper business as he moved on to Illinois and Kansas. Wells also telegraphed home and was relieved to learn that her sixteen-year-old sister Lily was fine. She arranged for Lily to move back to California.

Ida B. Wells realized that her days of living in Memphis—or anywhere in the South—were over. She took stock of her situation. She was in New York, the nation's largest city, without a home, a job, friends, or any money or clothes except what she had brought with her. Almost every dollar to her name had been tied up with the *Free Speech*.

T. Thomas Fortune came to her rescue. Feeling that having Wells on his staff would be a tremendous boost to the *New York Age,* he invited her to become one-fourth owner of the newspaper and to write a weekly column. As her thirtieth birthday approached, Ida B. Wells was about to begin a new life in the North.

5

"I Saw Them Burn the Nigger, Didn't I, Mama?"

TODAY ALL FAIR-MINDED people consider Ida B. Wells a heroine for exposing the truth about lynching. Edward Carmack, who called Wells a "black scoundrel" and stirred up hatred against her, is remembered as a bigot. In the late 1800s and early 1900s, however, few white southerners held these opinions. With black Tennesseeans deprived of the vote, Carmack was elected to the U.S. House of Representatives and then to the U.S. Senate. The former editor of the *Memphis Daily Commercial* became involved in a political dispute with another white man and died in a gunfight on the streets of Nashville in 1908.

Ida B. Wells was not only exiled from Memphis, she was also banished from history books about the city for many years. Two of the most famous works on Memphis history are *The Biography of a River Town*, a 1939 book by Gerald M. Capers, and *Memphis Down in Dixie*, a 1948 history by Shields McIlwaine. The first book praises the Ku Klux Klan for its "ability to control the Negroes." The second lionizes Nathan Bedford Forrest, chronicling in thirty-four pages his exploits as a Memphis slave trader, Confederate general, and organizer of the Ku Klux Klan. Neither of these Memphis histories makes even a single reference to Ida B. Wells by name, although Capers has one indirect reference: "No files have been preserved of the first Negro paper, the Memphis *Free Speech,* started by a woman in 1890, for its tone grew so militant that a mob burned its press."

A century ago it was unusual for an unmarried woman to begin a new life far from home where she had no family or friends. Ida undoubtedly felt very homesick in New York City, but she did not record her feelings. She had ended her diary five years earlier, in 1887, and her autobiography barely refers to her life in New York, not even disclosing where she lived. By 1892 she was no longer wrapped up in her own experiences and moods, for her days of "wondering what kind of creature I will become" were over. Tommie Moss's murder had involved her in the battle against lynching, which was rapidly becoming her all-consuming purpose in life. For many years hardly a day passed that she didn't devote to *Crusade for Justice,* as she called her life's work and titled her autobiography. When not writing, she lectured to whoever would listen—whether an audience of ten or ten thousand.

Within a week of her arrival in New York City, Wells was hard at work for the *New York Age*. She had brought her research notes with her, and she used them to write one of the most detailed articles on lynching up to that time. Published under the pen name "Exiled," Wells's article appeared on the front page of the *New York Age* on June 25, 1892. T. Thomas Fortune ordered ten thousand copies of the issue printed and distributed throughout the country. A thousand copies were sold in Memphis alone.

Five days later, on June 30, 1892, a white Memphis newspaper responded. "Since leaving Memphis," declared the *Appeal-Avalanche,* "she has gone to New York, where she is connected with a paper called *The Age,* in which she continues to publish matter not a whit less scandalous than that which aroused the ire of the whites just prior to her departure." But many other people were grateful to Wells for opening their eyes to the evil of lynching. Seventy-five-year-old Frederick Douglass left his home in Washington, D.C., and visited Ida to tell her that her article had been a "revelation" to him. While he had disapproved of lynching, Douglass confessed, he had assumed that the victims were guilty and weren't worth the time and effort of saving. If the greatest

Frederick Douglass

living black leader was so misinformed, Wells realized, then there must be millions of black and white northerners who didn't know the facts about lynching.

Perhaps at Douglass's suggestion, Wells decided to publish a pamphlet. Expanding upon material from her articles, she quickly wrote a manuscript called *Southern Horrors: Lynch Law in All Its Phases*. Wells couldn't find a publisher who would pay her for the right to print her pamphlet, for it didn't promise to be a moneymaking venture. So she had to finance its publication herself. To help her obtain the money, two hundred fifty women in New York City decided to hold a fundraising testimonial in her honor. On the night of October 5, 1892, hundreds of women and a few men from as far away as Philadelphia and Boston packed New York's Lyric Hall.

The testimonial was one of the most moving experiences of Ida's life.

Entering Lyric Hall, she saw her pen name, "Iola," spelled out in electric lights at the back of the stage. The programs the ushers handed to the audience were miniature copies of the *Free Speech*.

The evening began with music and speeches. As she sat on the stage awaiting her turn to speak, Wells was suddenly seized by panic. Although she had performed as a member of the Lyceum in Memphis and had spoken to groups while selling newspaper subscriptions, never in her life had she been called upon to deliver such an important address. It was crucial that she make a good impression, for the audience included many of the country's most educated and influential black women. Dr. Susan McKinney of Brooklyn, the nation's first black woman physician, had come to hear her, as had Gertrude Mossell of Philadelphia, a prominent newspaper editor and writer. The program was chaired by noted social worker Victoria Earle Matthews of New York. Frederick Douglass was unable to attend but was represented by his granddaughter's husband, C. S. Morris. Most of the audience had entered Lyric Hall assuming that lynching victims "got what they deserved," as Frederick Douglass had believed. If she could convince them of the truth, some powerful voices would be added to the anti-lynching movement.

Wells thought the best strategy with this well-educated audience was to present the facts dispassionately. Above all, she told herself, she must not make an emotional display. Called to the podium, she began reading a prepared speech, but not far into it, her worst fears came to pass. She was describing the murder of her friend Tommie Moss, and tears began streaming down her face. She asked for a handkerchief, wiped away her tears, and continued her talk, convinced that she had failed the cause that was so dear to her.

After her speech was over, C. S. Morris came up to Wells and said that her heartfelt words had profoundly stirred the audience. The women presented Wells with a gold brooch shaped like a pen and with a check for five hundred dollars. Wells wore the brooch over her heart for twenty years. She used the money to publish her pamphlet.

Just a month after the Lyric Hall testimonial, *Southern Horrors: Lynch Law in All Its Phases* was published. In the foreword, Frederick Douglass wrote:

> Brave woman! You have done your people and mine a service which can neither be weighed nor measured. If American conscience were only half alive . . . a scream of horror, shame, and indignation would rise to Heaven wherever your pamphlet shall be read.

The pamphlet chronicled numerous lynchings, including the murder of the three Memphis storekeepers. Wells also showed how southern white newspapers misrepresented the facts about lynching. She praised several southern officials, including Georgia Governor William J. Northen, for opposing lynching. In a concluding chapter she advised southern blacks to boycott businesses that practiced segregation and to move away from places that permitted lynchings.

Southern Horrors wasn't the only beneficial result of the Lyric Hall fundraiser. At the time, clubs were very popular. Towns had business, literary, and charitable clubs, ethnic clubs that preserved old-country traditions, and suffrage clubs that promoted women's voting rights. A few clubs, such as the Lyceum in Memphis, were for black women, and a few black women, such as Josephine St. Pierre Ruffin, participated in predominantly white clubs. By and large, however, black women had been excluded from the club movement.

After listening to Ida at Lyric Hall, Mrs. Ruffin invited her to speak about lynching to a group of black women at her home in Boston. This talk was another great success and gave Ruffin and Wells an idea. Together they organized the Women's Era Club of Boston, the first civic club for black women in the United States. With Josephine St. Pierre Ruffin as president, the Women's Era Club worked to end lynching and to promote civil rights.

Pleased with their success in Boston, Mrs. Ruffin arranged for Ida to speak to black women in several other Massachusetts and Rhode Island

SOUTHERN HORRORS.

LYNCH LAW

IN ALL

ITS PHASES

Miss IDA B. WELLS,

Price, - - - - Fifteen Cents.

THE NEW YORK AGE PRINT,
1892.

Title page of Southern Horrors

cities. Mrs. Ruffin accompanied Wells, and at the end of each speech they organized the women into a civil rights club. As Ida's fame spread, invitations poured in for her to speak in Washington, D.C., and in Pennsylvania and Delaware. Now and then Wells addressed white people, as well as audiences of both races. Pleased and a little surprised that white people were joining her crusade, she began to call lynching a "crime against humanity" that good people everywhere must work to end.

In November 1892 Wells addressed an integrated audience in Philadelphia. After the speech a white woman with an English accent told Wells she was shocked that Americans tolerated lynching. Her name was Catherine Impey, and she was visiting relatives in Philadelphia but would soon return to England, where she edited a magazine that championed the rights of the British-ruled people of India. Wells could not have guessed it, but Miss Impey would soon help her expand her anti-lynching crusade to an international stage.

When not on speaking tours, Wells continued to write for the *New York Age*. There was said to be a price on her head far beyond Memphis, so she could no longer travel in the South. Instead, she hired detectives to investigate lynchings. When she heard of a terrible incident in Paris, Texas, she hired a detective from the famous Pinkerton Detective Agency to go down and gather the facts.

The detective reported that in early 1893 a four-year-old white girl named Myrtle Vance was found murdered in the woods. Myrtle's father was a policeman in Paris, Texas, who had made many enemies by mistreating prisoners. Henry Smith, a black man arrested for drunkenness, was one of the prisoners he had beaten. A neighborhood handyman, Smith was a known alcoholic who was considered harmless. But when the police couldn't find clues regarding the child's murder, people in the area decided that Henry Smith must have committed the crime.

Henry Smith did not behave like a guilty man. He remained at home for a day or two after Myrtle's body was found. Once he learned that a mob was after him, however, he ran off, reaching Clow, Arkansas, more than one hundred miles to the east, before being captured.

The train returning Henry Smith to Paris, Texas, was met by more than ten thousand people. So many residents of Texas and Arkansas wanted to see Smith lynched that special excursion trains were chartered to carry spectators to Paris. Many other people arrived by wagon. In some towns the schools were let out so that children could come and witness the spectacle.

The "inhuman monster," as a newspaper called Smith, was placed on a carnival float, in mockery of a king upon a throne, and paraded through town. He was taken to a field and tied to a scaffold, where the men of the Vance family thrust red-hot irons down his throat and

The mob in Paris, Texas, as Henry Smith was paraded through town before being lynched

burned out his eyes. The only known objection came from a black minister named Reverend King, who told the crowd, "For God's sake, send the children home!" Reverend King was struck on the head with a rifle butt and run out of town.

Finding that Henry Smith was still breathing, the crowd poured oil on him and lit him on fire. Once his body was burned, onlookers fought over the hot ashes for his teeth, bones, and other souvenirs. Their thirst for blood unsatisfied, the mob seized a young man named William Butler and hanged him outside Paris. Butler had an excellent reputation but was killed merely because he was Henry Smith's stepson.

Charred body of Jesse Washington, eighteen-year-old African American lynched in Waco, Texas, in 1916

New York Age—Feb.18,1893

THE REIGN OF MOB LAW
Iola's Opinion of Doings in the Southern Field.

The lynching epidemic still rages in Texas. Gov. Hogg denounced the lynchers, who burned Henry Smith as murderers, telegraphed the District Attorney and sheriff of Lamar County, where the burning occurred, to discharge their duty and amke complaint and report those known to have been engaged in the lynching." ... The mob has so little fear and so great contempt of the Governor, the sheriff and the District Attorney that it went a few days later February 7th and lynched Will Butler.

Will Butler was a stepson of Henry Smith, the man who was burned alive, and made himself notorous during the search for Smith by claiming to know his whereabouts which he would not divulge"-- so said the dispatches. Hence , because Will Butler did not tell where his step-father was, he too was lynched. ...

New Orleans, Jan.21- A mob of masked men broke into the jail last night at Convent, St. Joseph Parish and forced the jailer to open the cells of Robert Landy and Pick George, who were incarcerated there, one for garroting and robbing a telegraph operator at Dehon Station and the other for murdering a man named Denhorst.

Both were taken to a shed and lynched. Our race still sits and does nothing about it and say little except to doubt the expediency of or find fault with the remedy proposed, \by which the things can be investigated, the country arpused and the temple of justice, the pulpit and the press besieged until public opinion shall demand a cessation of the reign of barbarism, lynch law and stake burning. No money and little support to give to this work, but some of our prominent men and women have put their names on a circular . asking the race to give entertainments on March 9, to raise money to defray the expenses of a most comfortable "day of praise at the World Fair August 17, to be known as "Afro American Jubilee Day."... Even if the condition

Original typewritten article "The Reign of Mob Law," in which "Iola" described the murders of Henry Smith and William Butler for the New York Age of February 18, 1893

More than a century later we still do not know if Henry Smith killed Myrtle Vance, for there was no trial. Some reports said he "denied everything," but the committee that seized him in Arkansas claimed that he confessed. Reverend King reported that Smith asked him, "Is it true, did I kill her?" as though he didn't know whether he had committed the crime.

A tragic effect of the Smith-Butler murders was that hundreds of young spectators were led to believe that lynching was acceptable. Ida B. Wells learned of a seven-year-old witness who was overheard bragging, "I saw them burn the nigger, didn't I, Mama?" "Yes, darling," answered her mother, "you saw them burn the nigger."

Wells described this and other lynchings in the *New York Age* and in another book she started writing. But she began to realize that lecturing and writing about lynching weren't enough and that the federal government might have to step in to end it. The problem was that by the late 1800s, northern lawmakers were reluctant to try to pass and enforce a federal anti-lynching law, for they feared that antagonizing the South might spark another Civil War. Wells wondered: How could pressure be exerted to involve the U.S. government in the anti-lynching crusade?

After returning to England, Catherine Impey continued to read about lynchings in America. She visited a friend, the Scottish author Isabelle Mayo, who, like herself, was interested in helping oppressed people. Miss Impey and Mrs. Mayo organized a group called the Society for the Brotherhood of Man and wrote Ida B. Wells a letter requesting that she or Frederick Douglass visit Britain to lecture about lynching. The society would pay traveling expenses.

When she received the letter, Wells was a guest in the Washington, D.C., home of Frederick and Helen Douglass. She showed Douglass the letter. After reading it, the famous leader said, "You go, my child. You are the one to go, for you have the story to tell."

Ironically, Wells had accomplished more to combat lynching while in

New York City than she had when living in the South, the scene of most of the crimes. Now she realized that she might accomplish even more in Great Britain, three thousand miles away across the ocean. Americans were strongly influenced by British public opinion. The two countries conducted a great deal of business with each other, and more Americans traced their roots to Great Britain than to any other part of the world. If British opinion could be marshaled against lynching, it might prod the U.S. government to act. Wells wrote back accepting Catherine Impey and Isabelle Mayo's offer.

She packed her notes and clothes and on April 5, 1893, set sail for England.

6

Light from the Human Torch

IDA B. WELLS EMBARKED on her voyage in high spirits. She shared a stateroom with Dr. Georgia Patton, Tennessee's first black woman physician. Heading to Africa as a medical missionary, Dr. Patton knew many of Wells's friends and told her news of home. Patton would later marry David W. Washington, a Memphis letter carrier who had once courted Wells.

In the diary the steamship company provided, Wells wrote that all went well on the first two days of the voyage. But then . . .

> Third Day: Seasick. So is Dr. Georgia Patton. We have a stateroom to ourselves and lie in the two lower berths looking at each other. Ugh.

> Fourth Day: Seasick still. Am afraid to lift my head. How I hate the sight of food.

> Fifth Day: Seasicker.

> Sixth Day: Seasickest. How I wish I was on land. Got better this evening after swallowing half the ship doctor's medicine chest contents.

On the ninth morning Wells awoke to find the vessel docked at Liverpool, England. After traveling to Catherine Impey's home in southern

England and spending a few days there to recover, Wells began her lecture tour. Accompanied by Impey and Isabelle Mayo, she delivered nearly fifty lectures during a six-week period—a rate of about a lecture a day. As one of the first African American women to speak in Great Britain, Wells drew large crowds and attention from the press wherever she appeared.

Her campaign began in Aberdeen, Scotland, where she lectured on lynching and segregation to an audience of fifteen hundred men. Similar talks followed in Glasgow and Edinburgh in Scotland and in Newcastle, Manchester, Birmingham, and London in England. She spoke at churches, clubs, public meetings, and gatherings of the Young Men's Christian Association (YMCA) and of the British Women's Temperance Union (BWTU), which worked to combat alcoholism and other social problems.

Everywhere she appeared, she was asked why she had traveled so far from home to speak about lynching. Each time she answered, as a newspaper quoted her: "Our own country remains silent on these continued outrages. It is to the religious and moral sentiment of Great Britain we turn. These can arouse the public sentiment of America so necessary for the enforcement of law."

She was interviewed by many prominent editors and reporters. The *Peterhead Sentinel,* a Scottish journal, condemned the American South for denying black people "all the rights of citizens" and declared that "freedom is mocked in the country that boasts itself the freest in the world." In Manchester the prominent newspaper *The Guardian* praised Wells's "brave and outspoken contention for justice." Under the headline LYNCH LAW IN AMERICA the *Birmingham Daily Post* reported: "Miss Wells argued that British public opinion, if properly aroused, would have good effect upon the people of the United States." The London journal *Society* reported that "A very interesting young lady" was visiting, "in the hope of arousing sympathy for the Blacks, whose treatment in the United States is not seldom fiendishly cruel."

After completing her lecture tour, Wells sailed for home around June 1. Before her departure either Catherine Impey or Isabelle Mayo informed her that news of the Henry Smith lynching in Paris, Texas, was what had prompted them to send for her. "The fire lighted by this human torch [Smith] flamed round the world," Wells wrote in her autobiography.

Wells returned home to a new racial controversy. On May 1, 1893, a world's fair opened in Chicago. Called the World's Columbian Exposition, it celebrated (a half year late) the four hundredth anniversary of Christopher Columbus's voyage to the New World in 1492. Many nations provided exhibits for the fair showcasing their people and achievements. President Benjamin Harrison of the United States had

The World's Columbian Exposition of 1893

not included a single black person among the more than two hundred planners of the American displays. As a result the American exhibits offered nothing relating to the country's black citizens. Frederick Douglass was the only African American to take part in the fair, yet not even he represented his nation. Douglass ran the exhibit for Haiti, an island country to which he had once served as U.S. minister.

Black leaders were appalled. In the thirty years since the slaves had been freed, black people had produced many authors, artists, inventors, scientists, and lawmakers. Moreover, seven and a half million of the country's sixty-three million people were black. How could the United States ignore the achievements of one eighth of its population? If nothing were done, the twenty-two million visitors from around the world who attended the fair might come away thinking that no black people lived in the United States.

Immediately upon her return to the States, Wells continued by train to Chicago to join a small group of black leaders who were determined to protest this injustice. They included Frederick Douglass and Ferdinand Lee Barnett, a Chicago lawyer who published *The Conservator*, the city's first black newspaper. Douglass, Barnett, and Wells decided to produce a pamphlet entitled *The Reason Why the Colored American Is Not in the World's Columbian Exposition*. Wells volunteered to compile and edit it, raise money for its publication, and have it printed.

During her stay in Chicago Wells visited black churches to speak about segregation and lynching and to raise money for *The Reason Why*. She also accepted Ferdinand Barnett's offer to work part-time as a reporter on his newspaper. Meanwhile, she asked Frederick Douglass to write an introduction for the pamphlet, the author I. Garland Penn to do a chapter on the achievements of black Americans, and Ferdinand Barnett, her employer at *The Conservator*, to write a chapter on the exclusion of black people from the world's fair. Wells wrote a chapter called "Lynch Law," which described the history of lynching as well as several grisly lynchings.

Within a few weeks Wells had raised five hundred dollars to publish *The Reason Why,* assembled and edited the material, and had twenty thousand copies printed. Originally she had intended to publish the entire pamphlet not only in English but also in French and German, but a shortage of time and money limited her to publishing only the preface in all three languages. Frederick Douglass provided Wells with a desk at the Haitian building, and all day for several weeks Wells passed out free copies of *The Reason Why* to visitors from around the world. Later, portions of the booklet were published in such places as Russia, Germany, France, and India.

The Haitian building was one of the fair's most popular attractions. Parents led their children there to shake hands with Frederick Douglass, who at more than seventy-five years of age was a living legend. Born a slave in Maryland around 1817, Douglass had escaped north as a young man. Among his many achievements he had published a famous autobiography, *Narrative of the Life of Frederick Douglass,* begun the anti-slavery newspaper *North Star,* and turned his home in New York State into a station on the Underground Railroad, the network of hiding places for escaped slaves.

Observing how people flocked to catch a glimpse of Douglass, and perhaps influenced by Ida B. Wells's pamphlet, the world's fair authorities finally decided to do something to honor African Americans. They asked Frederick Douglass to organize a Colored People's Day for August 25.

Wells felt that the U.S. government was just throwing black people a little something to appease them and advised Douglass to refuse the offer. Douglass listened to the thirty-one-year-old Wells, whom he sometimes addressed as "my child," and answered that half a loaf was better than no bread at all. Disappointed that Douglass wasn't more defiant, Wells refused to attend the Colored People's Day celebration.

The morning after the program, Wells read about it in the newspapers. Under Frederick Douglass's direction Paul Laurence Dunbar, a twenty-one-year-old elevator operator from Ohio, had read a selection from his poetry. Dunbar would later become one of the country's most famous poets. There had also been musical performances, and Douglass had given a powerful speech about the injustices suffered by black Americans.

Reading about all this, Ida felt her heart swell with pride. She rushed out to the fairgrounds and begged Douglass to forgive her for being a "hothead." Still, part of her must have remained convinced that she had been right, for to the end of her life she didn't believe in compromise or in accepting "half a loaf."

An interesting incident involving Wells and Douglass occurred near the close of the fair. One day "the grand old man," as Wells called him, stopped by the office of *The Conservator* and invited her to lunch. Once they reached the street, Douglass led her to the Boston Oyster House, but Wells pointed out that this Chicago restaurant did not serve black people.

"Come, let's go there!" said Douglass, taking hold of her arm.

Prepared to fight the way she had nine years earlier on the Chesapeake & Ohio train, Wells entered the restaurant on the arm of the distinguished-looking elderly black man. The waiters did not offer to seat them, so Douglass walked up to a table, pulled out a chair for his young friend, and then sat down. They were ignored for a while longer, but then the proprietor recognized Mr. Douglass and came forward to greet him cordially. Proud to have such a prominent man in his establishment, the proprietor ordered his waiters to take care of the gentleman and his guest.

While they were eating, Douglass said, "Ida, I thought you said they didn't serve us here. We are getting more attention than we want."

Wells realized that only Frederick Douglass's fame had enabled them to be served and that this was just a very small victory. Still, she enjoyed defying the policy of segregation, which in the North operated more by tradition than by law.

The World's Columbian Exposition closed on October 31, 1893, after running for six months. But instead of returning to New York City, Wells decided to make Chicago her new home. This midwestern city had a large black population actively involved in church and civic work. Chicago also appealed to her for a personal reason. After being courted by at least a dozen young men in Memphis and New York City, Wells had finally met a man whose affection she returned. He was Ferdinand L. Barnett, her boss at the newspaper and one of the co-authors of *The Reason Why*.

Ten years her senior, Barnett was a widower with two young sons. Wells and Barnett were an example of the expression "opposites attract." Barnett was tall and thin, while Wells was short and tended to be chubby. He had a Northwestern University law degree; she hadn't

Ferdinand Lee Barnett

been able to attend college. While she scraped to earn a living, he was well-to-do, with a successful law practice as well as his newspaper. He loved to cook; helping to raise her brothers and sisters as a teenager had given Ida a distaste for household chores. Moreover, she was fiery and intense, while he had a quiet sense of humor and a ready smile. One quality they shared was a passion for justice. Ferdinand was once threatened with jail for saying in a speech that the American flag was nothing more than a dirty rag if it didn't protect all its people, regardless of their color.

"Ida and Ferdinand were both ahead of their time," their granddaughter Alfreda Duster Ferrell explains. "In an era when most men expected women to stay at home and not speak out on social issues, Ferdinand accepted the fact that Ida was an activist and encouraged her in her work. This was one of the things that attracted her to him."

As Wells and Barnett worked together on *The Conservator,* their respect and love for each other grew. However, according to family legend, says their grandson Donald Duster, Ferdinand proposed marriage to Ida three times before she finally accepted. The couple agreed to marry in a year or two. Until then Wells intended to accomplish a great deal in her anti-lynching crusade.

In September 1893 Wells formed the first civic club for black women in Chicago. Soon it had more than three hundred members, ranging from the city's most prominent black women to high school girls. The group met weekly, and when Wells left Chicago on a prolonged speaking tour, the women voted to name it the Ida B. Wells Club in honor of its founder and president. One of the club's first projects was to raise funds to prosecute a Chicago policeman who had killed a black man. Later the Ida B. Wells Club would establish the city's first kindergarten for black children.

Meanwhile, Wells continued to gather material for another book on lynching. She called it *A Red Record,* because within its pages she chronicled some of the bloodiest lynchings she had encountered, including the murder of C. J. Miller, which had occurred at Bardwell, Kentucky, on July 7, 1893. It was said that Wells investigated the Miller case herself, posing as the dead man's widow in order to meet witnesses. It seems unlikely, however, that Ida would visit the southern state of Kentucky just a year after being threatened with death in nearby Tennessee.

On July 5, 1893, Mary and Ruby Ray, two white sisters, were found murdered not far from their home near Bardwell. The next day word reached Bardwell that a "strange Negro," C. J. Miller, had been caught hitching a ride on a freight train fifty miles away in Missouri. He was considered strange because he spoke intelligently and had fifteen dollars, a lot of money for a hitchhiker.

Thirty Kentuckians went to Missouri to fetch Miller, who was taken to Bardwell and jailed. The murdered girls' father believed Miller was innocent, because several witnesses had seen a white man fleeing the crime scene. But a mob formed, intending to lynch Miller. The crowd demanded: Wasn't that red spot on Miller's shirt blood? No, it was paint, Miller insisted. He said that his tormentors could take the shirt to an expert, and if the spot proved to be blood, they could kill him. The mob had no time for that. When he saw that he was to be pulled from jail, the prisoner said, "My name is C. J. Miller. I am from Springfield, Illinois. My wife lives at 716 North Second Street. I stand here surrounded by men who are excited, men who are not willing to let the law take its own course. I am innocent." Until then, he insisted, he had never been in Kentucky in his life, and on the day the murder had supposedly occurred, he had been in Bismarck, Missouri, more than a hundred miles from Bardwell.

Mr. Ray prevented the crowd from seizing Miller until three in the afternoon. But then the mob rushed the jail, stripped Miller of his clothing, and placed a metal chain around his neck. He was dragged through the streets, followed by thousands of people, many of them drunk. Convinced that they were about to kill an innocent man, Mr. Ray begged the mob not to lynch Miller. Ignoring him, they hoisted Miller to the top of a telegraph pole by the chain around his neck, then dropped him. The fall broke his neck. Shots were then fired into his body, his fingers and toes were cut off as mementos, and the corpse was burned.

A short time later a message reached Bardwell, via the same telegraph pole where Miller had been murdered. Someone had sent a telegram to Springfield to check Miller's story. Yes, came the response, Miller was an upstanding citizen who lived where he had said. Too late, the crowd realized that they had hanged an innocent man. Not one person was punished among the thousands who had taken part in the lynching of C. J. Miller.

Mob at Jesse Washington's lynching in Waco, Texas, in 1916

Two weeks later another awful lynching took place in Wells's old hometown of Memphis. Two white women were driving into town when a black man suddenly jumped into their wagon and demanded that they give him food from their basket. He was hungry and was desperate for something to eat. The women screamed, and the man, Lee Walker, ran away.

Word spread that a black man had tried to rape two white women. Mobs went out searching for Walker. While looking for him, they shot another black man dead because he didn't stop when ordered. After a few days Walker was captured and locked in the Memphis jail.

Ida B. Wells had proof that the Lee Walker lynching was planned at least ten hours in advance. On Saturday, July 22, 1893, a telegram arrived at her Chicago newspaper office daring her to come to Memphis to stop the lynching. Incredibly, this taunting telegram was sent by a white newspaperman:

> LEE WALKER, COLORED MAN ACCUSED OF RAPING WHITE WOMEN, IN JAIL HERE. WILL BE TAKEN OUT AND BURNED BY WHITES TONIGHT. CAN YOU SEND MISS IDA WELLS TO WRITE IT UP?
> ANSWER R. M. MARTIN WITH *PUBLIC LEDGER*.

Wells apparently didn't see the telegram in time. Otherwise she would have wired officials in Tennessee and perhaps even the president of the United States to try to prevent the lynching. Ten hours after the telegram arrived, on Saturday night, a mob pulled Lee Walker from his cell, as had been done to the three Memphis storekeepers the previous year. The "wretch-like demon," as a Memphis newspaper described Walker, was taken outside and hanged from a telephone pole in an alley. Then his body was burned. Such was Lee Walker's punishment because he had tried to scare two white women into giving him food. Once again the murderers went unpunished.

★

In late 1893 Ida B. Wells received an invitation from the Society for the Brotherhood of Man asking her to return to England. She agreed to go, then thought of a way to inform her readers about her travels. *The Conservator,* published by her fiancé, Ferdinand Barnett, was a weekly newspaper that paid her a small salary. The Windy City was also home to the powerful *Chicago Inter-Ocean,* a daily considered by Wells to be the nation's only white newspaper to consistently denounce lynching. Before leaving Chicago, she visited the *Inter-Ocean*'s office and asked its editor to hire her to write articles about her anti-lynching crusade in England. To her delight he agreed, making Wells one of the first black foreign correspondents for an American newspaper. But to her dismay she found that she didn't have enough money to travel abroad. Wells contacted her friend Frederick Douglass, who lent her twenty-five dollars that she promised to repay shortly after she began her speaking tour in England.

Wells departed Chicago in early 1894 and sailed from New York in February. On Friday, March 9, 1894, she landed in Liverpool, filled with hope that this trip would be even more successful than her first had been.

"A Work Which Nobody Else Will Do"

I DA B. WELLS KNEW that she wasn't easy to get along with. At twenty-three she had written in her diary that "I cannot or do not make friends" and admitted that she felt isolated from other people. "My temper has always been my besetting sin," she later wrote. She was also blunt and not at all diplomatic. People who did not support her anti-lynching crusade one hundred percent were part of the problem, she believed—and she told them so. Her refusal to compromise even slightly on matters of right and wrong often placed her at odds with her own friends and associates, making her what historian Thomas C. Holt called "a lonely warrior." Never was this more apparent than during her second trip abroad.

Her tour got off to a rousing start. The local leader of the Society for the Brotherhood of Man arranged for Wells to speak in Liverpool's Pembroke Chapel on Sunday, March 11, 1894, just two days after her arrival in England. The pastor, the Reverend Charles Aked, delivered his sermon and then announced that those who wanted to could stay to hear Ida B. Wells. Nearly all of the thirteen hundred people in the church remained to hear the American talk about the murder of C. J. Miller and other lynchings. While in Liverpool Wells stayed at the home of Reverend Aked and his wife, who became her dear friends. In her autobiography she acknowledged that they were among the first white people she knew with whom she felt comfortable:

They seemed to sense that I did not like, or rather had no confidence in, white people, and they set themselves to uproot my natural distrust and suspicion. The Queen of England herself could not have been treated with more consideration than I was during the whole course of my stay with them.

Wells soon encountered unexpected trouble, however. Her problems stemmed from a feud between Isabelle Mayo and Catherine Impey, organizers of the Society for the Brotherhood of Man.

One of the volunteers who helped raise funds and arrange meetings for the society was a dentist living in Scotland named Dr. George Ferdinands, who came from the island of Ceylon (now Sri Lanka), off the coast of India. Miss Impey fell in love with Dr. Ferdinands, and she wrote him a letter telling him so. Dr. Ferdinands admired Miss Impey but evidently did not return her love. Not knowing how to respond, he showed Miss Impey's letter to Mrs. Mayo.

Despite her talk about the "brotherhood of man," Mrs. Mayo was outraged and disgusted that her friend had fallen in love with an Asian man. She confronted Miss Impey with the letter and demanded that she withdraw from the Society for the Brotherhood of Man. Claiming that her romances were nobody else's business, Miss Impey refused. Mrs. Mayo informed other leaders of the society about the letter and succeeded in turning many of them against Miss Impey.

Mrs. Mayo demanded that Ida denounce Catherine Impey and cut off contact with her. Having seen many black men lynched for their love affairs with white women, Ida was probably the last person who would condemn an interracial romance. Besides, she did not like being told what to do. She informed Mrs. Mayo that she would neither criticize Miss Impey nor try to force her out of the Society for the Brotherhood of Man. It appears that she also told Mrs. Mayo that she should be ashamed of herself for attacking Miss Impey over a personal matter.

The society had agreed to pay Wells two pounds per week, which

GEORGIA—Continued

Oct. 1....DUNCAN, JOHN................Spring Place, Murry Co........Living with a white woman
   " 12....MOORE, WILLIAM................Jesup, Wayne Co................Throwing stones
Nov. 10....THOMAS, JOHN................Midvile, Burke Co................Rape
   " 16....ANTHONY, JOHN................Lincolnton, Lincoln Co..........Attempted rape
Dec. 26....JACKSON, PETER................Jesup, Wayne Co................Race hatred
   " 26....HOPPS, WILLIAM................Jesup, Wayne Co................Race hatred

1890

Feb. 28....BROWN, WASHINGTON........Athens, Clark Co................Rape
Mar. 24....MARTIN, SAMUEL................Wrightsville, Johnson Co........Murder
June 10....PRINCE, GEORGE................Elbert Co................Alleged rape
   " 10....POKE, JESSE................Eastman, Dodge Co................Murder
   " 10....PERRY, RICH................Marion Co................Unpopularity
   " 13....PENNER, GEORGE................Elberton, Elbert Co................Rape
   " 28....ROBERTS, ANDREW................Waycross, Ware Co................Rape
July 11....HARMON, JAMES................Social Circle, Walton Co........Rape
Oct. 12....WOSTEN, FRANK................Homer, Banks Co................Incendiarism
   " 24....WILLIAMS, JOHN................Waynesboro, Burke Co............Murder
   " 31....TWO NEGROES................Barton Co................Rape
   " 31....POLASCO, ——................Valdosta, Lowndes Co............Rape
Nov. 1....JONES, OWEN................Pulaski, Candler Co................Rape
   " 19....SIMMONS, JOHN................Cairo, Grady Co................Rape
Dec. 3....UNKNOWN NEGRO................Rome, Floyd Co................Unknown cause

1891

Feb. 21....KING, WESLEY................Locality undetermined............Murder
   " 26....WEST, ALLEN................Abbeville, Wilcox Co................Rape
July 1....BUCK, DANIEL................Bluffton, Clay Co................Rape
Aug. 29....OWENS, WILLIAM................Jesup, Wayne Co................Rape
Sept. 26....MACK, CHAS................Swainsboro, Emanuel Co............Rape
Nov. 2....*NIX, LARKIN*................Decatur Co................Murder
Dec. 16....GOLDEN, WELCOME................Waycross, Ware Co................Rioting
   " 14....KINGUT, ROBERT................Waycross, Ware Co................Rioting
   " 15....UNKNOWN NEGRO................Camak, Warren Co................Burglary

1892

Jan. 9....*NUX, ——*................Mitchell Co................Murder
Mar. 1....*JONES, ——*................Ware Co................Murder
Apr. 5....FIVE NEGROES (5)................Near Lithonia, Dekalb Co........Rape
   " 14....WEST, WILLIAM................Locality undetermined............Murder
May 17....THREE NEGROES (3)................Clarksville, Habershaw Co....Suspected robbery
   " 21....SMITH, SERBORN................Covington, Newton Co............Rape
June 11....MORELAND, ANDERSON........Forsythe, Monroe Co................Rape
July 21....UNKNOWN NEGRO................Jesup, Wayne Co................Supposed offense
Aug. 25....HOWARD, BENJ................Josselin, Liberty Co................Murder
Sept. 8....WILLIAMS, JESSE................Eastman, Dodge Co................Attempted rape
Oct. 26....WILSON, JAMES................Dalton, Whitfield Co............Race prejudice
Nov. 26....*SCOTT, GESTER*................Calhoun, Gordon Co................Murder
Aug. 30....JESSY, JOHN................Near Forsyth, Monroe Co........Rape

1893

Mar. 1....HILL, THOMAS................Spring Place, Murray Co........Rape
May 23....MUCHLEA, EPHRIM................Hazelhurst, Jeff Davis Co........Murder
   " 23....UNKNOWN NEGRO................Hazelhurst, Jeff Davis Co........Murder
July 17....DEAN, WARREN................Locality undetermined............Rape
Oct. 22....JENKINS, EDWARD................Clayton Co................Murder
Dec. 2....HOLT, LUCIUS................Concord, Pike Co................Murder
   " 19....FERGUSON, WILLIAM................Adel, Berrien Co................Turning State's evidence
   " 25....THOMAS, CALVIN................Locality undetermined............Unknown offense

1894

Feb. 10....COLLINS, ——................Athens, Clarke Co................Enticing servant

One of sixty-three pages of NAACP lynching statistics for the years 1889–1918; note the reasons for lynching.

was equal to about ten U.S. dollars in 1894 and had the buying power of about two hundred dollars today. This was virtually the only income she could expect in Great Britain, aside from her modest salary from the *Chicago Inter-Ocean.* Through Mrs. Mayo's influence the society cut off most of the salary Wells had been promised. Moreover, the society did not schedule the extensive speaking tour Wells had anticipated. Mrs. Mayo offered to resume her support if Wells would change her mind and denounce Miss Impey, but Ida held firm.

Three thousand miles from home, with little money and fading prospects for speaking engagements, Wells wasn't sure where to turn. Reverend Aked said that if she could obtain a letter from a prominent American describing her anti-lynching work, it would enable her to meet influential English people and arrange her own speaking tour. Wells immediately thought of her friend Frederick Douglass, who had encouraged her to visit Britain the first time when he said, "You are the one to go, for you have the story to tell." Nine days after arriving in England, Wells wrote a letter to Douglass explaining her predicament:

> Liverpool, Eng.
> March 18, 1894
>
> Dear Mr. Douglass,
>
> I arrived safely Friday of last week and have already addressed an audience of 1300 persons. I find quite to my surprise that Mrs. Mayo is hostile because I will not consent to a denunciation of poor Miss Impey and will therefore have no part in the work. As Miss Impey is practically retired because of what I told you, I am compelled to depend on myself somewhat. . . . I am visiting at the home of Rev. C. F. Aked, the most popular pastor in Liverpool with the largest congregation. It was at his church I spoke. He thinks that I should have a letter of introduction from you. Please write one as soon as you get this and forward to me immediately. You know about my work and can the better com-

mend me to these forces than I can speak for myself. Indeed
I should be most glad if you will write Mr. Aked himself. . . .
Trusting to hear from you soon, I remain, yours affectionately,

Ida B. Wells

Wells didn't know it, but Mrs. Mayo had also written to Frederick
Douglass. She apparently accused Wells of interfering in the Impey
matter and of coming to England uninvited. This attempt to turn Douglass against Wells partially succeeded, especially since he was peeved at
Ida anyway. Wells had sent the twenty-five dollars Douglass had lent her
to California to buy such things as school supplies for her sisters Annie
and Lily. Because her salary from the Society for the Brotherhood of
Man was cut off, Wells couldn't repay Douglass as soon as she had
expected. Someone—perhaps Mrs. Mayo—suggested to Douglass that
Wells had taken advantage of his generosity.

Had they lived today, Wells and Douglass could have set the facts
straight in a transatlantic telephone call. That was not possible in 1894.
Instead, seventy-seven-year-old Frederick Douglass questioned whether
Wells was entirely trustworthy. Little-known letters preserved among
the Ida B. Wells Papers at the University of Chicago Library and at the
Library of Congress in Washington, D.C., reveal that Douglass and
Wells had a rather serious quarrel across the ocean.

For the sake of her anti-lynching campaign, Douglass promptly
answered Wells's request for a recommendation. From his home in
Washington, D.C., he sent a typewritten letter to Reverend Aked:

Cedar Hill, Anacostia, D.C.
March 27th, 1894

Rev. C. F. Aked,

Dear sir,

Miss Ida B. Wells, now sojourning in England, known to
me by the persecutions to which she had been subjected on

account of her bold exposures of southern outrages upon colored people, has told me of the kindness and help she has received at your hands, at the beginning of her present mission to England. I join with Miss Wells in thanking you for opening the doors of your church, and otherwise assisting her in obtaining a hearing in England. . . .

I deem it highly important to the cause of justice and humanity, that the English people should know the truth concerning the outrages committed upon colored people in the southern states of the Union. . . . I am glad that you now have in England, one so competent as Miss Wells, to tell the negro's side of this story of race persecution.

If I were a few years younger, I would willingly join Miss Wells in her work. . . .

Very truly and gratefully yours,
Frederick Douglass

On March 27, the same day that he sent this recommendation, Douglass wrote Wells a personal letter with a very different tone. In it he expressed grave doubts about her integrity. "If you have not been invited and have gone to England on your own motion and for your own purposes, you ought to have frankly told me so," Douglass chastised her. "I am ready to hold up your hands, and want to [help you], but I wish to do so intelligently and truthfully."

Upon receipt of this letter, Wells might have been wise to calmly explain to Douglass that Mrs. Mayo had drawn her into the dispute and had cut off her income, but she viewed Douglass's doubts as a personal attack and a hindrance to her anti-lynching work. Wells wrote Douglass a blistering eight-page reply that began:

Manchester, April 6th, 1894

Dear Mr. Douglass:—

Your letter which I received this morning has hurt me cruelly. With all the discouragements I have received and the time and money I have sacrificed to the work, I have never felt so like giving up as since I received your very cool and cautious letter this morning with its tone of distrust and its inference that I have not dealt truthfully with you. . . .

Regarding the money, she promised to repay it as soon as she could, explaining that "I am left to my own resources practically, because I will not consent to [condemn] poor Miss Impey. Mrs. Mayo could and would [restore her assistance to Wells] if I would agree to her plans regarding Miss Impey. That I never will do even if I must beg my way home." She went on to say that she felt lonely doing "a work which nobody else will do," but that "I welcome gladly every opportunity to spread the truth and shall continue to do so as long as I am here." She closed by saying:

> While my heart bleeds that you should class me with that large class who have imposed upon your confidence, I still love you as the greatest man our race has yet produced and because of what you have suffered and endured for the race's sake. . . .
>
> Ida

But she wasn't finished. A month later she sent Douglass another letter berating him for not providing her with a more supportive recommendation. She had not expected him to "gush" about her, she explained, but it would have been "better if you had spoken more positively regarding me and my work," because many people "don't know whether to take my word or not that lynching is so terrible a thing." She added that "What I want is that the people here shall know that 12 Negroes have been lynched the past 2 weeks and nothing is being done about it, and that an expression of opinion from them would have great weight."

Nonetheless, Frederick Douglass's letter must have been of some help, for she was able to arrange dozens of speaking engagements in front of many tens of thousands of people in England. In Liverpool she spoke ten times on the topic "Lynch Law in the United States," with each engagement averaging about a thousand listeners. Moving on to Manchester, she spoke twelve times in ten days, and in Southport she addressed a gigantic audience of two thousand persons. Every few days she sent an article to the *Chicago Inter-Ocean* for her series, which was headlined IDA B. WELLS ABROAD.

The outpouring of support from the clergy, lords and ladies, and the public prompted Wells to become bolder in her articles. In a piece about her visit to Bristol, where she spoke twice a day for a week, she declared, "Our American Christians are too busy saving the souls of white Christians from burning in hell-fire to save the lives of black ones from present burning in fires kindled by white Christians."

Wells completed her four-month lecture tour in London, one of the world's great cities. She met members of Queen Victoria's cabinet, visited Parliament, presented numerous talks, and was interviewed by about twenty newspapers and magazines.

A number of U.S. newspapers reported on Wells's travels through England, gathering their information from the *Inter-Ocean* and from British journals. In the South, where a black person couldn't walk on the same sidewalk or use the same bathroom as a white, African Americans were proud to learn of Ida B. Wells's enthusiastic reception in England. Many whites were incensed, however. The *Memphis Daily Commercial* called Wells a "Negro adventuress" and concocted a lie that she had been the lover of Reverend Taylor Nightingale, her former business partner at the *Free Speech*. Even some northern newspapers criticized her for inviting the English to "meddle with our affairs," as the *New York World* claimed.

There was a further complication in London when Wells clashed with one of the world's most influential women. Frances E. Willard, an American temperance (anti-alcohol) worker, was in England at the same time as Wells. President of the American Woman's Christian

Temperance Union (WCTU), Willard was the guest of Lady Henry Somerset, a leader of the temperance movement among British women.

Ida B. Wells disliked Frances E. Willard. During a tour of the American South, Willard had been entertained by what she called "the best white people" and had apparently adopted their racist views in order to gain their support. In a *New York Voice* interview in 1890 Willard had said: "The grogshop [tavern] is the Negro's center of power. Better

Frances E. Willard

whiskey and more of it is the rallying cry of great, dark-faced mobs. The colored race multiplies like the locusts of Egypt. The safety of [white] women, of childhood, of the home is menaced in a thousand localities."

Wells kept a copy of this article in her purse. Whenever she was asked her opinion of Willard at one of her lectures, she would read it aloud and question why Willard had said nothing about drunken white mobs who threatened black Americans. Wells also criticized Willard in several of her *Inter-Ocean* articles.

Wells and Willard were both invited to speak before a group of British temperance workers on May 9, 1894. Nearly everyone expected Wells to be polite to Willard, who was twenty-three years her senior and who had been nicknamed by British editor W. T. Stead "the Uncrowned Queen of American Democracy." However, when addressing the audience, Ida complained about influential white women who did nothing to stop lynching—an obvious slam at Willard. In addition, she arranged for Willard's *New York Voice* interview to be reprinted in *Fraternity,* the journal published by the Society for the Brotherhood of Man. That way thousands of British people could learn about the temperance leader's racist views.

Frances Willard and her hostess, Lady Somerset, were enraged by Wells's attack. Lady Somerset informed Wells by telephone that, if the issue of *Fraternity* were distributed, she personally would prevent Wells from being heard further in Britain. Lady Somerset also sent a transatlantic cablegram to Frederick Douglass demanding that he publicly reprimand Wells.

Although it must have seemed to him that Wells was quarreling with *everyone,* Douglass refused to give in to Lady Somerset's demand. Ida B. Wells distributed the magazine, and Willard and Lady Somerset failed completely in their effort to discredit her. Historian Dorothy Sterling wrote about this incident: "For an unknown black woman to tackle the famous Frances Willard was a little like David facing up to Goliath with a slingshot." In her autobiography Wells wrote: "This attack was not only a boomerang to Miss Willard, it seemed to appeal to the British sense of fair play. Here were two prominent white women, joining hands in the effort to crush an insignificant colored woman who had neither money nor influence—nothing but the power of truth with which to fight her battles."

Backing down somewhat, Frances Willard arranged for Lady Somerset to interview her for the *Westiminster Gazette*, a London newspaper, so that she could clarify her views. In this interview Willard spoke of the "profound horror which everybody must feel in the presence of such cruelty [lynching]," and criticized "half-drunken white roughs who murder them [black people] at the polls or intimidate them so they do not vote." But Willard repeated her assertion that "the best people I knew in the South" assured her that black people "menaced the safety of women and children." She added that "it is not fair that a plantation

Anti-lynching demonstration in England

Negro who can neither read nor write should be entrusted with the bal-lot." Unwittingly, Willard had revealed herself to be the bigot Wells had said she was, and lost much of her support in England.

Meanwhile, Ida B. Wells continued to lecture to large audiences in London. She was honored with a dinner in Parliament, and just before her departure she achieved one of the greatest triumphs of her anti-lynching crusade. She helped organize the London Anti-Lynching Committee, which included dozens of the most prominent editors, ministers, college professors, members of Parliament, and lords and ladies in Britain. The committee was headed by the Duke of Argyle, whose son was married to Queen Victoria's daughter. To show that she was on the side of justice, Lady Henry Somerset also joined the com-mittee.

Her work finished in London, Wells said good-bye to her English friends. In July she sailed for home, eager to see the effect her four-month crusade in England had generated across the Atlantic.

"A Special Call for Special Work"

IDA B. WELLS ARRIVED in New York in late July 1894. She returned to the States having learned a great deal about obtaining support from influential people and forming organizations to help her crusade. Before settling permanently in Chicago, she decided to travel across the country lecturing and forming anti-lynching groups similar to the London Anti-Lynching Committee.

Her first big meeting was at the Academy of Music in Brooklyn, New York. She noticed a change in her listeners from the start. Pressure from British newspapers, which had called the United States uncivilized for allowing lynching, had sparked a greater interest in her crusade than ever before. The audience at the Brooklyn Academy of Music was as disturbed by her lynching stories as any group she had addressed in England.

American newspapers now interviewed Ida regularly and sent reporters to her lectures, especially since she was becoming more outspoken. Previously, she had been reluctant to mention that some white women were romantically involved with black men. This was a touchy subject, even in the North. Now she openly told newspaper reporters that young black men were lynched simply because they had white girlfriends.

The *New York Sun* scheduled a major interview with Wells for August 3. A day or two before, a delegation of black men visited her. They said that they were proud of her work but asked her to "soft-pedal" her comments about black-white romances because it would antagonize many well-meaning white people. Wells refused, saying that as long as men were called rapists and were lynched for what were actually romances between consenting adults, she must tell the truth.

In Philadelphia Wells shared the stage with Frederick Douglass. The two of them had patched up their differences, and Wells apparently repaid the money Douglass had lent her. During a stop in Chicago her fiancé, Ferdinand Barnett, organized a standing-room-only talk for Ida at Quinn Chapel AME Church. In Cleveland she attended the WCTU's annual convention, again sharing the stage with Frances Willard. The two women maintained their mutual dislike. Wells had hoped to convince the WCTU to pass an anti-lynching resolution, but, as she wrote, "that great Christian body which expressed itself in opposition to card playing, saloons, and tobacco, wholly ignored seven million colored people whose plea was for a word of sympathy and support."

In Rochester, New York, Wells was invited to stay in the home of Susan B. Anthony, the renowned leader in the fight for women's suffrage. The seventy-four-year-old "Susan B." admired Wells's fiery style and became her friend, but she offered one criticism: Wells should avoid clashes with people like Frances Willard, because women would gain more by sticking together. Anthony illustrated her point with a story about how, for the sake of the struggle for women's voting rights, she had once behaved much like Willard.

During the early days of the suffrage movement, Anthony explained, Frederick Douglass had been one of the few men to attend their meetings and promote their cause. Douglass was made an honorary member of the National Woman Suffrage Association, of which Anthony was president. But when a suffrage convention was held in Atlanta, Georgia, Susan B. Anthony asked Douglass not to attend, because a black man's presence would offend white southerners. Not only that, added Anthony, but when a group of black southern women asked her

Susan B. Anthony

to help them form a suffrage group, she refused, once again because it might antagonize southern whites.

"And do you think I was wrong in so doing?" Miss Anthony asked her guest.

Without hesitation, Wells answered, "Yes!"

"When women get the ballot," Anthony replied, using one of her favorite lines, "all that will be changed."

Wells didn't agree with that, either. "Miss Anthony, do you really believe that the millennium is going to come when women get the ballot? I do not believe that the exercise of the vote is going to change [people's nature] or the political situation."

The famous suffragist seemed a bit startled by Wells's boldness, but the two women nevertheless became close friends. At one of Wells's talks in Rochester, a southern man in the audience sarcastically asked, "If the colored people are so badly treated in the South, why don't more of them come North?" Before Wells could respond, Susan B. Anthony leaped to her feet and said, "I'll answer that question! It is because we in the North do not treat the Negroes any better than they do in the South, comparatively speaking."

For a year Wells crisscrossed the country, traveling to Missouri, California, Kansas, and Nebraska. Everywhere she went, she organized anti-lynching groups, convincing many thousands of people to join her crusade.

In November 1894 she spoke in Providence, Rhode Island. Frederick Douglass came from Washington, D.C., to attend this rally, and he helped attract a "monster meeting," as Wells called especially huge gatherings. Waiting together in a little room before they took the stage, Douglass asked her, "Ida, don't you feel nervous?"

"No, Mr. Douglass," she responded.

"For the fifty years that I have been appearing before the public I have never gotten over a nervous feeling before I have to speak," he confessed to her.

"That is because you are an orator, and naturally you are concerned as to the presentation of your address," Wells responded. "With me it is different. I am only a mouthpiece through which to tell the story of lynching and I have told it so often that I know it by heart."

The "monster meeting" in Providence was the last time she would ever see Frederick Douglass, whom she had called "the greatest man our race has yet produced" and whom she considered the closest thing she had had to a father (complete with arguments) since her parents' death. Three months after that meeting, while Wells was in San Francisco, Frederick Douglass died at his home in Washington, D.C., at the age of seventy-eight.

As she traveled by train between cities, Wells continued to work on *A Red Record,* a meticulously researched 115-page work that included lynching statistics for 1892, 1893, and 1894 and detailed many specific cases. One heart-rending case involved the Hamp Biscoe family, hard-working farmers who lived near Little Rock, Arkansas.

Falsely claiming that Hamp Biscoe owed him a hundred dollars, a white man tried to seize the Biscoes' little farm as payment. To protect his property, Biscoe fired a gun at a white law officer, wounding him slightly. The officer fired back, wounding Biscoe in the head so seriously that he was expected to die.

Instead of trying to save Biscoe, a white mob locked him, his pregnant wife, and their thirteen-year-old son and baby in a small frame house. At night about fifteen men stormed the house. Mrs. Biscoe began to cry, "You intend to kill us and take our money!" The men told her to hush, they had come to give her a present. The "present" was a flurry of bullets, which killed her and her husband immediately. Seeing that the thirteen-year-old son was wounded but alive, a man placed a pistol against his chest and shot him again. Still, the youth lived long enough to tell neighbors what had happened as well as the names of the attackers. The infant, shot in the face, was the only survivor.

"Perhaps the civilized world will think," Wells wrote, "that this matter was duly investigated, the criminals apprehended, and punishment meted out to the murderers. But this is a mistake. Nothing of the kind was done or attempted." Despite being identified by Hamp Biscoe's dying son, the murderers were left alone by legal authorities.

In June 1895 Wells returned to Chicago, where she had *A Red Record* published, again paying for the printing with funds she had raised. The book featured pictures of lynching victims—images so gruesome that they brought home the reality of the situation to readers. To help with

This political drawing from 1901 shows that lynching destroys justice.

Judge Lynch's Latest Victim.

her crusade in Chicago, Wells formed the Central Anti-Lynching League, which, along with the Ida B. Wells Club, distributed *A Red Record* to humanitarian groups around the world. Wells sent free copies of *A Red Record* to those who couldn't afford to buy it.

The summer of 1895 was a happy one for Ida. At eight o'clock on the night of June 27 she and Ferdinand Lee Barnett were married before an overflowing crowd at Chicago's Bethel Church. The bride, who was three weeks shy of her thirty-third birthday, wore a white satin gown trimmed with orange blossoms. Her sisters Annie and Lily came from California to serve as bridesmaids. Following the ceremony, hundreds of people attended a reception held by the Ida B. Wells Club to honor the newlyweds.

The marriage was unusual by the standards of a century ago. To begin with, the bride refused to give up her birth name. She was one of the first married women to hyphenate her name, becoming known as Ida B. Wells-Barnett. Secondly, a few days before their marriage, Ida and her husband-to-be made a business deal. Ida purchased Barnett's newspaper, *The Conservator,* and became its publisher, editor, and business manager. The newlyweds had no honeymoon. They were married on a Thursday night, and early Monday morning Wells-Barnett headed to *The Conservator's* office on Chicago's State Street to take over its operation.

A copy of The Conservator *while under Ferdinand Barnett's editorship*

THE CONSERVATOR.

F. L. BARNETT, Editor.

ALEX. G. CLARK, Managing Editor.

A. CLARK, General Traveling Agent.

CHICAGO, SEPT. 8, 1883.

Societies and socials desiring to be reported in the CONSERVATOR must send tickets to this office in reasonable time. Hereafter we shall make mention of no meetings unless this requirement is complied with.

SPECIAL NOTICE.

All subscribers who change their Residences must be certain to send us notice of their new location. Failure to do so will seriously injure our prompt delivery and cause many subscribers to miss their Saturday Conservator.

CITY NEWS.

—Fall

—Is here.

—Lay in coal.

—Pity the poor oyster.

—Bring us your job work

—Schools all in full blast.

—Preachers have got to work again.

—Bethesda Church Fair opens in October.

—Have you had the Hay fever?

—The Dime Museum is worth twice the admission.

—The Hyers Comedy Combination is an undoubted success.

—Watch for the Garfield Singers at Bethesda Church.

—The Chicago Union Base Ball Club has disbanded.

—President Arthur was bridged Tuesday. The beautiful Chicago

jumped out but the painter was not quick enough. His head was caught between the elevator and the floor and his life was literally crushed out. The poor man left a widow and four small children.

—The Christian Aid Association gave another of its interesting concerts at Bethesda church Monday night. The audience was large and appreciative. The features of the evening were, excellent singing by the association, Mrs. Powell and Miss Rosa Colman, readings by Mr. Murphy and Mrs. Nellie Douglas Horn. The former rendered his inimitable "woman's rights", winning an encore. Mrs. Horn read "Little sister and I" and received a double encore. The proceeds of the evening were very encouraging and the church acknowledges many obligations for the assistance rendered by this very generous organization.

—Mr. and Mrs. Wm. H. Curd, 2926 Butterfield street, invited a few friends to spend a social evening with Miss Meta Pelham, of Detroit and Miss Mary Tomlinson, sister of the hostess, last Saturday. By 8 o'clock, nearly every guest had honored the notice and the parlors were well filled. Music and parlor games became the order of exercises and continued throughout the evening, varied by a collation well served. At the close sincere regrets were expressed that Miss Pelham, who was on the eve of leaving for her school in Hannibal, Mo., was obliged to cut short her visit to this city.

THE BLACKVILLE TWINS.

The Hyers Comedy Combination opened the season at the Criterion Theatre, Monday night, to a crowded house. It was a distinction shown to this troupe by giving them the

Mrs. T. B. Leonard, of Buffalo N. Y., is in the city, the guest of T. F. Dyson, 230 4th ave.

Miss Fannie Richards of Detroit Mich., returned home Friday, th ult., having spent a fine visit her countless friends in the Ga city.

Mrs Sarah J. Bond, 2714 Dear st., accompanied by her daug left the city Aug. 25th, to visit tives in Baltimore and Washing

After an enjoyable visit to fri in this city, Miss Nellie Banks for Kansas City last Saturday.

Misses Sophia and Fred Jones, both brilliant colored scho continue their studies this year at University of Michigan.

Miss Annie H. Jones pa through the city Friday of last en route for a year of school at Jefferson City, Mo.

Rev. T. L. Smith of Keoktk was in the city during the w He left for home Wednesd

Dr. Jas. E. Henderson retu to the city Monday, after a ten d visit to Waukesha and other plea resorts. He is much improved health by his trip.

Miss Emma Dixon, who has a guest of the Misses Jones, 595 ton st., returned to her home M day.

Rev. Jas. A. D. Podd i takin short vacation trip to Detroit, Mi leaving Wednesday P.M. A seige of severe work entitles hi a season of rest.

Mrs. Emma Barber, of Roche Ind., spent two weeks in the visiting her relative, Capt. R. Moore, 2962 Butterfield st.

The couple lived at 2939 South Princeton Avenue, about a half mile from *The Conservator*'s headquarters. Upon her marriage Ida became the stepmother of two young boys, eleven-year-old Ferdinand Jr. and nine-year-old Albert. However, she didn't have much to do with raising the boys, for her mother-in-law lived with them and ran the household. That suited Ida, for she wasn't bogged down with housework and could maintain her anti-lynching activities.

Few people expected Wells-Barnett to have children of her own. Thirty-three was well past the age when women of the 1890s generally began families, and it also seemed unlikely that she would let motherhood interfere with her work. Once again Ida surprised just about everyone, giving birth to a son on March 25, 1896. She and her husband named him Charles Aked Barnett after Reverend Charles Aked, her host during her second trip to England. Ida soon gave birth to another son, Herman, in 1897, and later to two daughters, Ida Jr. and Alfreda, in 1901 and 1904. Despite being a devoted mother, she managed to continue her anti-lynching crusade.

Because she nursed Charles, she brought him with her to the newspaper office and often took him to her political meetings. In the summer of 1896 a convention of delegates from black women's clubs was held in Washington, D.C. The Ida B. Wells Club chose its founder to attend. Wells-Barnett boarded the train with her baby and headed to the nation's capital.

Many prominent women attended the convention, including Margaret Murray Washington, wife of Booker T. Washington, the educator who founded Alabama's Tuskegee Institute, and Rosetta Douglass Sprague, daughter of Frederick Douglass. But the stars of the convention were its oldest and youngest attendees.

The oldest person at the gathering was seventy-six-year-old Harriet Tubman, who had led three hundred slaves to freedom along the Underground Railroad and who had served as a Union spy during the Civil War. The audience was mesmerized as this legendary woman

Ida and her first-born child, Charles, photographed when he was not quite a year old

related some of her exploits and sang an old Civil War song. Tubman then swept Charles Aked Barnett out of his mother's arms, carried him onto the stage, and presented him to the cheering delegates as "the Baby of the Convention."

Like most black people after the Civil War, Wells-Barnett supported the Republicans, the party of Abraham Lincoln. After returning to Chicago she was asked by the Women's State Republican Committee to tour Illinois on behalf of the party's nominee for president, William

Harriet Tubman

McKinley, as well as local Republican candidates. While working for the Republican ticket, she could also address audiences on such subjects as lynching, segregation, and voting rights.

She would be happy to tour Illinois making political speeches, she said—if the committee paid for baby sitters while she traveled about with Charles. The committee agreed, and off she went with her six-month-old baby. She spoke in such Illinois towns as Bloomington, Quincy, Decatur, and the state capital, Springfield.

At each stop a baby sitter watched over Charles at a house or hotel while his mother spoke. But in one town the baby sitter was so eager to hear Wells-Barnett that she sat with little Charles right on the stage.

When Charles heard his mother's voice, he threw a fit, as babies will when they see and hear their mothers but can't reach them. The chairwoman of the meeting had to carry Charles out into the hall so that the baby sitter could hear the rest of the speech. Wells-Barnett often referred to this incident in later talks, saying, "I honestly believe I am the only woman in the United States who ever traveled throughout the country with a nursing baby to make political speeches."

Now that she was a mother, Ida's attention turned to schools. In the late 1800s the United States didn't have very many kindergartens, and kindergartens for black children were even rarer. Wells-Barnett realized that kindergarten would help children do well in school later on. Around the time that her second child, Herman, was born, she led the Ida B. Wells Club in establishing Chicago's first kindergarten for black children. The pastor of Bethel Church allowed the kindergarten to be held in his church's lecture room. Soon the kindergarten was filled with neighborhood children.

With Herman's birth, in November 1897, Wells-Barnett felt that she could no longer maintain her civil rights activities. "I had found that motherhood was a profession by itself, just like schoolteaching and lecturing," she wrote in her autobiography. She gave up her newspaper and resigned from the presidency of the Ida B. Wells Club. She had no intention of staying away from public life forever, but with a newborn baby and a twenty-month-old toddler, she focused her full attention on her family.

In the six years since the lynching of the three Memphis storekeepers, the situation had improved somewhat. Lynching had given the United States an international reputation for lawlessness. American industrialists who wanted to do business abroad condemned lynching, as did a growing number of American newspapers and statesmen. Most important, the public outcry against lynching was growing. Although a campaign to pass a federal anti-lynching law had failed, between 1893 and 1897 five southern states enacted such laws.

From a record high of 230 reported lynchings in 1892, the number decreased over the next five years to 152 (1893), 192 (1894), 179 (1895), 123 (1896), and 158 (1897). More than eight hundred lynching murders in five years was still shameful, but the trend was generally moving in the right direction. Much of the credit belonged to Ida B. Wells-Barnett and the campaign she had waged through her articles, books, lectures, and trips abroad.

A friend of hers, Bishop Henry McNeal Turner of the AME Church, lauded her accomplishments. "She has shaken this country like an earthquake," he wrote. "In the future she will be reverenced as the heroine of her race and vocabularies will be searched to write her praises in prose and poetry." Victor-Ernest Rillieux, the French-speaking poet from New Orleans, wrote a poem about her that began *"Tout pour l'humanité! tout pour Dieu! rien pour soi!"* ("All for humanity! all for God! nothing for herself!"). But Wells-Barnett wasn't finished. Her "retirement" from public life lasted only five months.

The federal government was more willing than private industry to employ black workers, although it often assigned African Americans to the most menial and lowest-paid jobs. One black man named to an important position was Frazier B. Baker, who was appointed postmaster of Lake City, South Carolina, in February 1898.

Whether in a large city or a small town like Lake City, the job of postmaster is respected to this day. But white people in the area were angry that a black man was running the town's post office. They tried to force Baker to quit by threatening him and his family. When that didn't work, they decided to kill him. On February 22, 1898—George Washington's birthday—a mob approached the Baker home in the dead of night. The lynchers set fire to the house and waited.

As the family ran to escape the flames, the mob fired their guns. Baker and the infant son he was carrying were wounded so severely that they fell into the fire and burned to death. Mrs. Baker and the couple's other five children escaped the burning house. However, all six of them were shot and wounded.

What distinguished this case was that Frazier B. Baker had been a federal employee, and so his murder deserved the attention of the U.S. government. Meetings were held around the country to discuss ways of involving the U.S. government in the case, not just the South Carolina authorities. At a mass meeting in Chicago money was collected to send someone to Washington, D.C., to present a demand for justice. Ida B. Wells-Barnett was selected to go.

Again, a nursing baby accompanied Ida, although this time it was five-month-old Herman. Once in the nation's capital, she met with seven members of the U.S. House of Representatives from the Chicago area and a U.S. senator from Illinois. These lawmakers arranged for her to speak to President William McKinley at the White House.

The president knew that Wells-Barnett had worked in Illinois to help his election, and he listened politely to her plea. "Nowhere in the civilized world save the United States do men go out in bands to hunt down, shoot, hang, or burn to death an individual," she told the president. "Postmaster Baker's killing is a federal matter, pure and simple. He died at his post the same as a soldier on the field of battle." Not only should the federal government punish the murderers, she insisted, but the president should suggest federal legislation "to outlaw the national crime of lynching."

The president pledged to do all he could to locate and punish the lynchers and said that the government had assigned some of its best Secret Service agents to the case. But President McKinley wasn't particularly known for his civil rights concerns. Besides, the United States was just then becoming involved in the Spanish-American War, which occupied the president and Congress far more than the postmaster's murder. Wells-Barnett remained in Washington, D.C., for more than a month, but the federal government did little to pursue the Baker case. Eventually, eleven men were tried in a federal court in South Carolina for the attack on the postmaster and his family. However, the jury was unable to reach a decision, and the accused men were set free.

President William McKinley

On April 21, 1898—around the time that Wells-Barnett and her baby returned to Chicago—the United States went to war with Spain. Thousands of African Americans sympathized with the goal of the Spanish-American War, which was to free Cuba from Spanish rule. But in many cases black men who volunteered to fight were turned away or assigned to cooking or cleanup details.

Ida felt that black men who wanted to serve should have the same opportunities as white men. She and other Chicagoans organized one of the few black fighting units of the war, the Eighth Illinois Infantry. When the unit went to Springfield for basic training in July, Wells-Barnett took both her young sons down to the Illinois capital and did volunteer work in the camp hospital and office. She remained with the Eighth Illinois Infantry to provide moral support until the soldiers left for Cuba.

The United States won the war in August. A short time later T. Thomas Fortune of the *New York Age* contacted Ida. He wanted her to come to Rochester, New York, to help organize a new civil rights group he was creating, the National Afro-American Council. Leaving Charles and Herman at home with her husband and mother-in-law, Wells-Barnett headed east to Rochester to stay at the home of Susan B. Anthony and attend the conference.

Wells-Barnett immediately felt a coldness from her friend Susan B. Anthony, who was now nearly eighty years old. Every time they spoke, Anthony called her "Mrs. Barnett," with a sarcastic emphasis on *Mrs.,* instead of Ida. Finally, Wells-Barnett asked her hostess, "Miss Anthony, don't you believe in women getting married?"

The famed suffragist must have been awaiting this question, for she snapped, "Oh, yes, but not women like you who had a special call for special work. I know of no one in all this country better fitted to do the work you had in hand than yourself. Since you have married, agitation has practically ceased. Besides, you have a divided duty. You are here trying to help form this league and your baby needs your attention at home. You are distracted over the thought that maybe he is not being looked after as he would be if you were there, and that makes for a divided duty."

Miss Anthony was wrong, for Wells-Barnett was about to stir up a great deal of agitation. In fact, she helped spark a debate that has continued among black leaders to this day.

The National Afro-American Council was formed, in part, in

response to a U.S. Supreme Court ruling of two years earlier. The infamous *Plessy v. Ferguson* decision of 1896 stated that racial segregation was legal. This unfortunate decision placed the U.S. government's seal of approval on the separation of the races that the South had instituted.

By 1898 black Americans were dividing into two groups regarding segregation and other racial issues. One group was led by Booker T. Washington, who had become the nation's most influential black leader following Frederick Douglass's death in 1895. Called conservatives, accommodationists, gradualists, or Bookerites, they believed in Washington's position that blacks should accept segregation to keep the peace, while gradually winning the acceptance of white America by educating themselves and working hard.

The other group, known as the radicals, militants, or anti-Bookerites, believed that black people shouldn't have to earn the approval of white America. This country belonged to black people as much as to white people, they claimed, so African Americans had the right to demand justice and equality. In more recent times this way of thinking has led to the Black Power movement.

Nearly all white people favored Booker T. Washington's teachings. In October 1898 President William McKinley invited Washington to dine with him in the White House, demonstrating that the U.S. government preferred black leaders who accepted segregation over those who "made trouble," as many whites phrased it. Most black people also feared that demanding justice would just get more African Americans killed, and felt that Washington's ideas were the most practical.

Wells-Barnett, described by a writer of the time as "a flame of righteous indignation," was perhaps the most militant member of the National Afro-American Council's organizing convention. Elected secretary of the council, she condemned Booker T. Washington for agreeing with Jim Crow policies and stunned nearly everyone by opposing the election of T. Thomas Fortune as council president. Although Fortune was her old friend and had organized the convention and invited her to it, Wells-Barnett felt that a more militant president was needed.

Booker T. Washington

She convinced the convention of her view and persuaded Fortune to turn down the position. In his place a more militant candidate, Bishop Alexander Walters of the AME Zion Church, was chosen president.

On November 10, 1898, shortly after the formation of the National Afro-American Council, eleven black people were killed in a terrible riot in Wilmington, North Carolina. President McKinley said nothing about the killings in a subsequent address to Congress, and, as with the murder of Postmaster Baker, he did little to involve the federal government in the case.

A month after the Wilmington riot the National Afro-American Council met in Washington, D.C. Wells-Barnett gave a rousing speech in which she condemned President McKinley for failing to punish the Wilmington rioters, criticized Booker T. Washington for accepting Jim Crow policies, and blamed herself for encouraging black soldiers to fight in the Spanish-American War when the United States failed to protect its own black citizens. "If this gathering means anything," she said, "it is that we have at last come to a point where we must do something for ourselves—and do it now! We must educate the white people out of their two hundred and fifty years of slave history."

Several council members who worked for the federal government and owed their jobs to President McKinley or to Booker T. Washington tried to shout Wells-Barnett down, calling her a "hothead." But she had a few supporters, and they hissed and booed her critics.

Before the meeting closed, the council issued an "Address to the Nation," which was a compromise between the militants, such as Wells-Barnett, and the Bookerites. It condemned President McKinley for ignoring lynchings, yet accepted "legitimate voting restrictions," including educational qualifications, that were used to exclude black voters.

Wells-Barnett was bitterly disappointed that black leaders were willing to compromise on matters of right and wrong. She didn't yet realize it, but by becoming more militant, she was moving far ahead of her time and was making enemies not only among white bigots and government officials but also among her own people.

"Mother, if You Don't Go, Nobody Else Will!"

R OBERT REED CHURCH, who had helped Ida pay for her return to Memphis from California in 1886, had a daughter named Mary. The South's first black millionaire, he had provided his daughter with the best of everything. Mary graduated from Ohio's Oberlin College, then went to Europe to study French, German, and Italian. Mary Church Terrell became known as the most educated black woman in the United States. She taught Latin at the Colored High School in Washington, D.C., and in 1895 became the first black woman on that city's Board of Education. As famous in her own right as Wells-Barnett, Terrell, in 1896, founded a civil rights organization called the National Association of Colored Women.

Mary Church Terrell and Ida B. Wells-Barnett differed in many ways. Terrell was a wealthy socialite who vacationed on the island of Martha's Vineyard, Massachusetts, and who had had marriage proposed to her by a German baron. Wells-Barnett knew how to talk the language of the streets, and she regularly visited the Joliet prison outside Chicago to speak with the inmates about their troubles. Terrell was the picture of ladylike refinement, while Wells-Barnett reportedly continued to keep handy the pistol she had bought after Thomas Moss's death—in case her old enemies from Memphis threatened her family. Perhaps the biggest difference was that Terrell supported the ideas of Booker T. Washington, while Wells-Barnett was one of the nation's most militant black leaders.

Mary Church Terrell

Yet the two women also had much in common. Both devoted their lives to helping their people. In addition both were from Memphis, and they had been acquaintances as young women. In an 1887 diary entry Wells had written: "Miss Church . . . is the first woman of my age I've met who is similarly inspired with the same desires, hopes, and ambitions. I was greatly benefited by my visit and only wish I had known her long ago." Because of all they had shared, Wells-Barnett was especially hurt by something Terrell did in 1899.

That summer Terrell called for a convention of the National Association of Colored Women to be held in Chicago. She did not invite Ida to this gathering of prominent black leaders, even though she lived in the city. Wells-Barnett knew that this was no oversight—that Terrell wanted to show the world she was distancing herself from the militant "troublemaker." Over the next few years Wells-Barnett would find herself increasingly isolated from black leaders who shared Terrell's opinion of her. In fact, for the rest of her life Wells-Barnett would be spurned by many who considered her too militant. Yet she refused to allow her hurt feelings to stand in the way of her work.

The turn of the century was a busy time for Ida. In 1899 a series of lynchings occurred around Palmetto, Georgia, near Atlanta. It began in March, when nine black men were arrested on suspicion of being involved in burning several buildings. As they awaited trial, the accused men were held in a warehouse in Palmetto. At one o'clock on the morning of March 16, more than one hundred masked men broke into the warehouse, overpowered the guards, and began shooting the prisoners. The mob killed five of them and wounded the others. Nothing was done about this mass lynching.

About a month later a black man named Sam Hose, also known as Sam Holt, was accused of killing his white employer near Palmetto. Rumors spread throughout the Atlanta area that Hose had murdered Alfred Cranford in cold blood and had raped Mrs. Cranford. A prominent newspaper, the *Atlanta Constitution,* whipped its readers into a frenzy by offering a five-hundred-dollar reward for Hose's capture and suggesting that he be burned at the stake.

Sam Hose was captured on the night of April 22. Georgia Governor Allen Candler did nothing to protect Hose, even though it was common knowledge that he would be lynched. Hose's captors took him to Newnan, a nearby town. As word spread that Hose would be lynched after church on Sunday, April 23, 1899, thousands of people flocked to Newnan by carriage and excursion train. At the appointed time, Sam Hose was tied to a pine tree, tortured, and then roasted to death. The

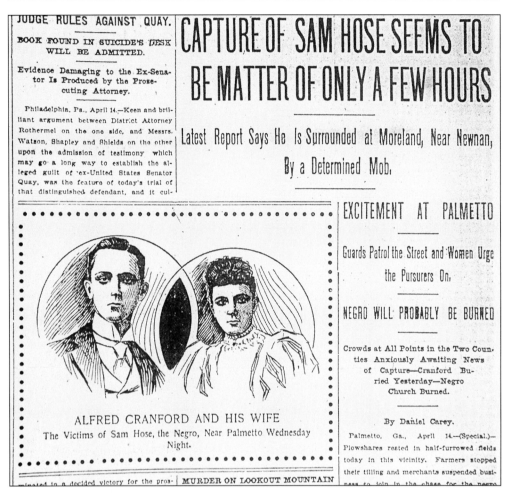

JUDGE RULES AGAINST QUAY.

BOOK FOUND IN SUICIDE'S DESK
WILL BE ADMITTED.

Evidence Damaging to the Ex-Sena-
tor Is Produced by the Prose-
cuting Attorney.

Philadelphia, Pa., April 14.—Keen and brilliant argument between District Attorney
Rothermel on the one side, and Messrs.
Watson, Shapley and Shields on the other
upon the admission of testimony which
may go a long way to establish the alleged guilt of ex-United States Senator
Quay, was the feature of today's trial of
that distinguished defendant, and it cul-

CAPTURE OF SAM HOSE SEEMS TO BE MATTER OF ONLY A FEW HOURS

Latest Report Says He Is Surrounded at Moreland, Near Newnan, By a Determined Mob.

ALFRED CRANFORD AND HIS WIFE
The Victims of Sam Hose, the Negro, Near Palmetto Wednesday
Night.

EXCITEMENT AT PALMETTO

Guards Patrol the Street and Women Urge
the Pursuers On.

NEGRO WILL PROBABLY BE BURNED

Crowds at All Points in the Two Coun-
ties Anxiously Awaiting News
of Capture—Cranford Bu-
ried Yesterday—Negro
Church Burned.

By Daniel Carey.

Palmetto, Ga., April 14.—(Special.)—
Plowshares rested in half-furrowed fields
today in this vicinity. Farmers stopped
their tilling and merchants suspended business to join in the chase for the negro

minated in a decided victory for the pros- | MURDER ON LOOKOUT MOUNTAIN

The Atlanta Constitution *predicted that Sam Hose (also known as Sam Holt) would be burned when caught . . .*

dead man's heart and liver were cut into pieces and sold for ten cents a slice by enterprising vendors.

Palmetto residents were disappointed that Sam Hose had not been lynched in their town. A rumor spread that before dying he had impli-cated a black preacher named Elijah Strickland in Cranford's murder. On Sunday night a mob broke into Strickland's cabin, pulling him from his wife and five children. A noose was tied around his neck and swung over a persimmon tree outside Palmetto. Three times Reverend Strick-

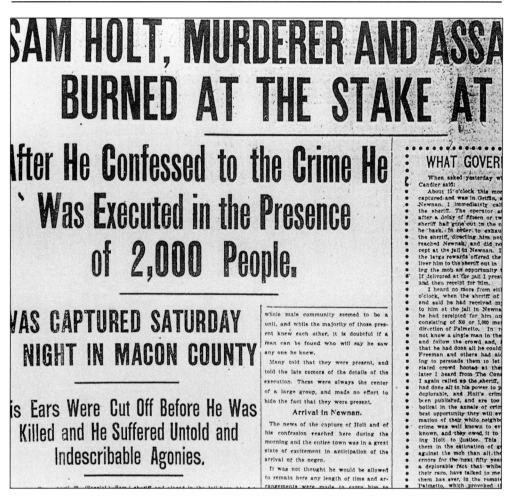

SAM HOLT, MURDERER AND ASSA
BURNED AT THE STAKE AT

After He Confessed to the Crime He Was Executed in the Presence of 2,000 People.

WAS CAPTURED SATURDAY NIGHT IN MACON COUNTY

is Ears Were Cut Off Before He Was Killed and He Suffered Untold and Indescribable Agonies.

whole male community seemed to be a unit, and while the majority of those present knew each other, it is doubtful if a man can be found who will say he saw any one he knew.

Many told that they were present, and told the late comers of the details of the execution. These were always the center of a large group, and made no effort to hide the fact that they were present.

Arrival in Newnan.

The news of the capture of Holt and of his confession reached here during the morning and the entire town was in a great state of excitement in anticipation of the arrival of the negro.

It was not thought he would be allowed to remain here any length of time and arrangements were made to carry him to

WHAT GOVER

. . . which was exactly what happened.

land was raised off the ground and then let down with the warning that he would die unless he confessed to helping to kill Cranford. Each time he proclaimed his innocence. The mob then raised him by the neck one final time, strangling him to death.

An arrest was made in the Hose-Strickland lynchings, but it wasn't of one of the lynchers. An elderly white Atlanta man, W. E. Pharr, was overheard saying that Sam Hose might have been lynched unjustly. A policeman arrested Pharr, who was locked up for "using language likely to cause disorder or a riot." Meanwhile, the lynchers went unpunished.

Together with other black Chicagoans, Wells-Barnett hired a Chicago detective named Louis P. Le Vin to investigate the lynchings. Le Vin spent more than a week in the Palmetto area. He later reported to Wells-Barnett: "There was no disposition [by area whites] to conceal any part they took in the lynchings. They discussed the details of the burning of Sam Hose with the freedom which one would talk about an afternoon's [entertainment] in which he had very pleasantly participated."

After speaking to many people, Le Vin concluded that Sam Hose had killed Alfred Cranford in self-defense. Hose had requested some of his back wages so that he could visit his sick mother. Cranford had refused to pay him. One day when Hose was chopping wood for Cranford, the two men began arguing. Cranford drew a gun, evidently intending to shoot Hose, who threw his ax, striking and killing Cranford. Hose did not rape Mrs. Cranford but fled to the woods, where he hid until he was captured. Hose never implicated Reverend Strickland in the killing. In fact, Le Vin reported that "I saw many [white people] who knew Strickland, and all spoke of him in the highest terms." The minister, who had been nearly sixty years old, had been murdered because the mob had been in a lynching mood.

As for the black men who had been shot in the warehouse, Le Vin reported: "It seems that one or two barns or houses had been burned, and it was reported that the Negroes were setting fire to the buildings. Nine colored men were arrested on suspicion. They were not men of bad character, but quite the reverse. They were intelligent, hard-working men, and all declared they could easily prove their innocence."

Wells-Barnett wrote a short pamphlet about these incidents, *Lynch Law in Georgia,* which appeared in 1899. It was followed by a longer work, *Mob Rule in New Orleans,* published in 1900. Most of the later pamphlet described a race riot in New Orleans that was touched off when policemen attacked a black man named Robert Charles for "talking sassy." In addition it described a number of lynchings, including that of Sam Hose.

Among Ida's readers was Congressman George H. White of North Carolina, who for a time was the only black member of the U.S. House of Representatives. In February of 1900 Congressman White rose to make an impassioned plea against lynching before his fellow lawmakers. He said that since the Civil War "fully fifty thousand of my race have been murdered by mobs"—more than ten times the usual estimates. He described the lynchings of Sam Hose and the men in the warehouse, and finished by proposing that Congress pass an anti-lynching bill to "protect all citizens of the United States against mob violence." Congressman White read his bill aloud:

> All . . . citizens of the United States are entitled to and shall receive protection in their lives from being murdered, tortured, burned to death by any and all organized mobs commonly known as "lynching bees." . . . Whenever any citizen or citizens of the United States shall be murdered by mob violence . . . all parties participating, aiding, and abetting in such murder and lynching shall be guilty of treason against the Government of the United States, and shall be tried for that offense in the United States courts.

Prolonged applause followed Congressman White's speech. But no federal anti-lynching bill was enacted—then or ever. Most southern lawmakers opposed such legislation. Northerners feared that sending federal troops into the South to prevent lynchings might provoke a second Civil War. Still, Ida's pamphlets and Congressman White's speech contributed to a rise in anti-lynching sentiment among many Americans.

Also around the turn of the century Ida fought a battle closer to home. The *Chicago Tribune* ran a series of articles calling for the establishment of segregated schools in the city. The articles featured interviews with parents who had withdrawn their children from a class taught by a black teacher and with southern whites who favored segregated schools. No black people were interviewed, nor was there mention of communities with successful integrated schools.

One Saturday afternoon Ferdinand Barnett came home from his law office complaining about one of the articles. "The *Tribune* is trying to abolish the mixed school system of Chicago, and I would be willing to wager that within five years it will achieve its object," he told his wife.

"What do you propose to do about it?" Ida responded. "Surely you are not going to sit still and allow such a thing without making some effort to prevent it."

"What can we do?" asked Ferdinand, knowing that if he irritated his wife enough, *she* would do something about it.

"That is exactly what we should find out," Ida told Ferdinand. "There must always be a remedy for wrong and injustice if we only know how to find it."

Once his wife used phrases like "wrong and injustice," Ferdinand knew that she was hooked. Ida sat down and wrote a letter to the *Tribune*'s editor, Robert W. Patterson, pointing out that everyone had been asked his opinion of segregated schools except those who would be stuck with an inferior educational system: Chicago's black people. She requested that Mr. Patterson meet with a delegation of black leaders to hear their views.

Many days passed, and her letter did not appear in the *Tribune*'s Voice of the People section. Suspecting that Patterson was ignoring her, she went to the newspaper office to speak to him. When he walked in and saw a plump, middle-aged black woman waiting for him, he said, "I have nothing for you today."

"What do you mean?" she asked, and then explained who she was.

"Oh, I'm sorry," he replied. "I thought you were one of the women from one of the colored churches coming to solicit a contribution, as they very frequently do."

Wells-Barnett laughed and said, "It seems natural that whenever you see a colored woman she must be begging for her church. I am begging, Mr. Patterson, but not for money." She briefly explained her views on the injustice of segregated schools.

Patterson not only disagreed with her, he insisted that ignorant Negroes shouldn't have the right to vote or to decide matters for white people just because they were in the majority in certain areas. Mr. Patterson had a winter home in Georgia, and Wells-Barnett saw that, like Frances E. Willard, his sympathies lay with the southern whites. She countered that he was as wrong to generalize about black people as she would be to condemn the entire white race just because some whites were ignorant. Finally Mr. Patterson snapped, "I do not have time to listen to a lot of colored people on the subject!"

"And they can't afford to waste their time in fruitless discussion with you!" answered Wells-Barnett, going out the door. But she wasn't finished with trying to prevent Chicago's schools from becoming segregated.

She went to a telephone and called someone whose opinion would influence the school authorities more than Patterson's: Jane Addams. In 1889 this famous social worker had founded a settlement house in a poor Chicago neighborhood. Called Hull House, it helped needy people with food, housing, and education. "Miss Addams, plenty of people in Chicago would not sanction such a move [segregated schools] if they knew about it," explained Wells-Barnett. "Will you undertake to reach those of influence who would be willing to do for us what we cannot do for ourselves?"

Addams agreed, and she arranged for a conference of influential people to meet at Hull House on the following Sunday. Wells-Barnett attended the meeting along with newspaper editors, ministers, a rabbi, a prominent lawyer, a judge, and several social workers. A man from the Chicago Board of Education was also there and admitted that a movement was afoot to segregate the city's schoolchildren.

"Would you use your power," Wells-Barnett asked the people at the conference, "to help us, your weaker brothers, secure an equal chance here in Chicago for children of all races?"

The lawyer rose and suggested that a committee be appointed to visit the *Tribune* to explain that Chicagoans wouldn't stand for segregated schools. A committee of seven people, headed by Jane Addams, visited the *Tribune* and spoke to Robert W. Patterson. Responding to their pressure, he discontinued the articles promoting segregated schools, and separation of the races in Chicago schools as a matter of policy was avoided.

Ida had a personal stake in the public schools. Her third child was born in 1901. She and Ferdinand named the little girl Ida Jr. Another daughter, Alfreda, was born three years later. By then the couple's first two children, eight-year-old Charles and seven-year-old Herman, had started school.

The Barnett children had an interesting and unusual childhood. Years later they said that their mother always seemed to be writing at the dining-room table, which was usually stacked high with magazines and papers. They became accustomed to seeing their mother's name in the newspapers and to meeting famous people. Carter G. Woodson, founder of Black History Month, visited their home, as did William Monroe Trotter, editor of the *Boston Guardian* and one of the few black leaders of the time as militant as Wells-Barnett. Paul Laurence Dunbar, who had become a well-known poet following the World's Columbian Exposition, was another friend. He would visit the family and read his poems to them. But you didn't have to be famous to be welcome in the Barnett home. Ida and Ferdinand often came to the aid of poor, jobless people who had moved to Chicago from the South in the hope of making a better life. Over the years they invited many homeless people to join their family for a home-cooked Thanksgiving dinner.

Just as Ida had grown up in Holly Springs, Mississippi, hearing her father and his friends talking about the Ku Klux Klan, the Barnett children grew up in Chicago listening to stories about segregation and

Jane Addams at the fortieth-birthday celebration of Hull House

Ida with her children in 1909. Charles is left, Herman right, Ida Jr. between the boys, and Alfreda in front.

lynching. But on one occasion Wells-Barnett managed to inject humor into a case of bigotry—no easy accomplishment! She was shopping in a Chicago department store where the clerks refused to wait on her because she was black. Taking a pair of men's underpants from a shelf, she draped it over her arm and headed toward the door as though not intending to pay. Suddenly a clerk appeared, asking, "May I assist you?" She told "the story of Dad's underpants" over and over to her children, and it always made them laugh.

Ida was a fiercely protective and demanding parent. A bunch of white ruffians known as the Thirty-first Street gang terrorized young black people in the Barnetts' neighborhood. One night the gang chased Charles and Herman home, threatening to beat them to a pulp. Hearing the commotion, Wells-Barnett came out and dared the gang to come fight her. Everyone in the neighborhood knew that Mrs. Barnett kept a gun somewhere in her house. The thugs ran away and left her sons alone after that.

Wells-Barnett was one of those parents who visit their children's schools so often, they seem to be on the faculty. When she was out of town, Ida telephoned to make sure the children were keeping up with their homework. Even after they entered high school, Ida refused to wait until parents' night to check on their progress. She would drop in to talk to their teachers, and as Alfreda recalled in an interview in 1976, when she was seventy-two years old, "the report had better be good!"

Togetherness was important to the Barnett family. Many nights the family took turns playing a four-person card game called whist. Ida and Ferdinand bought an old piano and gave their children music and dancing lessons. The family would gather around as the children showed off the latest pieces and dance steps they had learned. The Barnetts also had a Victrola, a hand-cranked record player. They listened to opera recordings and marched around the house to such songs as "Alexander's Ragtime Band." Ida's personal favorite was a humorous record called "The Preacher and the Bear," about a minister who went out hunting when he should have been in church. Cornered by a bear, the preacher prays: "Now, Lord, if you can't help me / For goodness' sake, don't you help that bear." She played this record again and again, and every time she heard it she laughed as hard as she did when telling the story of the underpants.

On Sundays, after church, the Barnetts visited Aunt Annie, Ida's sister who had settled in Chicago and founded a newspaper called the *Searchlight* with her husband. The children were fascinated when their mother and Aunt Annie spoke about slavery, the time their grandfather James Wells refused to vote the way old man Bolling ordered, or the terrible yellow fever epidemic of 1878.

When she was traveling, Ida sometimes wrote letters to her family. In the fall of 1920 she toured Illinois speaking at churches and at state institutions for the blind, deaf, and mentally ill. On Saturday, October 30, she became lonely for her family and wrote them a long letter that still exists. In it she expressed regret that "I won't be home to help my girls celebrate Halloween," even though her daughters Ida and Alfreda were already nineteen and sixteen years old. "I am so sorry about this as I wanted to be with you," she added. She promised to "reach home in time for dinner Monday night with my loved ones" and concluded by expressing how much her family meant to her:

> Whenever I think of my dear [family], which is all the time, such a feeling of confidence comes over me. I have had many troubles and much disappointment in life, but I feel that in you I have an abiding joy. Mother's heart is glad and happy when she thinks of her [children], for she knows that wherever they are and whatever they are doing they are striving to please her. With the earnest hope that you have a good time [on Halloween] and with love to all, I am,
>
> With all the love in the world,
> Mother

Ida with her sister Annie (middle); also pictured are (from left) Ida's daughters, Alfreda and Ida Jr., and her son Herman.

Charles, Herman, Ida Jr., and Alfreda realized that in one way their mother did not practice what she preached. They knew that she hated cooking and housecleaning and often heard her complain, "What's the use of dusting the house if you just have to do it again tomorrow? It doesn't accomplish anything." Although Ida baked bread, Ferdinand put on his apron and did most of the cooking. Yet despite her distaste for housework, Ida insisted that her children learn how to cook and wash and iron clothes. "You should know how these things should be done because you may have to do them one day," she would tell them.

Her biggest flaw as a parent was that she was at times overbearing. Although Alfreda was eager to go away to college, her mother refused to allow her to leave home and enrolled her at the University of Chicago. After Herman married, Ida fixed up part of her house so that her son and his wife, Fione, could remain with the family.

Charles, her oldest child, involved her in one of her greatest achievements. While the majority of lynchings were perpetrated in the South, some mob murders occurred in the North. In 1905 Wells-Barnett had promoted an anti-lynching bill for Illinois. The bill, which called for the removal of any sheriff who didn't do all he could to prevent a lynching, passed and was signed into law. In 1909 Illinois' anti-lynching law was tested under tragic circumstances.

In Cairo, in the southernmost tip of Illinois, the body of a white woman was found in an alley. Lacking clues, the police looked for someone on whom to pin the crime. They settled upon a penniless black man known as "Frog" James, who was arrested and locked up in the police station.

When a mob gathered around the station, Alexander County Sheriff Frank Davis was summoned. Sheriff Davis took James out into the woods, supposedly to hide and protect him, but the mob tracked down the sheriff and his prisoner and brought James back to Cairo. The lynchers hanged Frog James from an electric light pole, fired hundreds of bullets into him, and cut off his head. Not only did Sheriff Davis allow the lynching to occur, he may have been involved in it. Two men who had been hunting in the woods allegedly reported that the sheriff had sent a signal to inform the mob of the prisoner's whereabouts.

At first Illinois Governor Charles S. Deneen did not plan to hold Sheriff Davis responsible. Only when Ida B. Wells-Barnett and other black leaders sent Deneen telegrams reminding him of the law did he oust the sheriff from office. However, the new law also granted the sheriff the right to come before the governor and show why he should be reinstated. News reached Chicago that Davis would soon appear before the governor, asking for his job back. He planned to bring along prominent character witnesses, so his reinstatement seemed certain.

On the Saturday night four days before Davis's hearing, Ferdinand and Ida talked about the case at the dinner table while the children listened. "And so," Ferdinand told his wife, "it would seem that you will have to go to Cairo and get the facts with which to confront the sheriff next Wednesday morning. Your train leaves at eight o'clock."

This was one case in which Ida didn't want to get involved. She didn't mind traveling to Cairo to gather the facts and then to Springfield to present them to the governor. But she felt that she wasn't the right person for the case. What was needed was a lawyer—someone who thoroughly knew the law and could argue convincingly before the governor.

Three men lynched in Duluth, Minnesota

Ferdinand was a lawyer. However, he didn't think he could do the job, nor had he been able to find another lawyer willing to tackle what seemed like a hopeless assignment.

Ida picked up her youngest child, Alfreda, and carried her upstairs to bed. As was her habit, she sang her daughter to sleep, falling asleep herself in the bed alongside the five-year-old girl.

An hour or so later Wells-Barnett was awakened by her oldest child, thirteen-year-old Charles. "Mother," Charles said somberly, "Pa says it is time to go."

"Go where?" she asked.

"To take the train to Cairo."

"I told your father downstairs that I was not going," his mother responded.

Charles stood by the bedside awhile, staring at her. Then he said, "Mother, if you don't go, nobody else will!"

Ida nearly burst into tears. "Tell Daddy it is too late to catch the train now, that I'll go in the morning," she told her son. "It is better for me to arrive in Cairo after nightfall anyway." The next morning Ferdinand and their four children accompanied her to the train station and saw her off on her trip to southern Illinois.

She spent two days in Cairo talking with the black townspeople. Located just across the border from Kentucky, Cairo in some ways seemed to belong to the South more than to the North. Its black citizens were so scared to say anything against Sheriff Davis that a number of them had written to the governor requesting the sheriff's reinstatement. Wells-Barnett called a meeting of black townspeople and convinced them that they must be brave and sign a resolution condemning the sheriff for permitting the lynching. She persuaded a ministers' meeting to sign a similar resolution. Armed with the two resolutions, she boarded the train for Springfield.

On Wednesday morning at ten o'clock Wells-Barnett entered the state capitol, where the hearing was to take place. She was the only black person in the room. Frank Davis sat confidently facing her, accompanied by his lawyer (who was a state senator), a clergyman, and several politicians and friends who had come to testify as to his good character.

The hearing began, and Wells-Barnett listened as one man after another praised Sheriff Davis. His lawyer read dozens of letters and telegrams from bankers, lawyers, doctors, and newspaper editors requesting that Davis be returned to his position as sheriff. After the lawyer finished, Governor Deneen said, "I understand Mrs. Barnett is here to represent the colored people of Illinois."

Wells-Barnett rose from her chair with a look of surprise on her face, for until that moment she hadn't realized that the entire case would depend on her presentation. She faced the roomful of people who had come in support of Sheriff Davis and began talking. She spoke for several hours, presenting evidence that the sheriff had done nothing to stop the lynching and showing the governor the resolutions signed by the black people in Cairo. Finally, she ended by saying: "Governor, the state of Illinois has had too many terrible lynchings within her borders within the last few years. If this man is sent back, it will be an encouragement to those who resort to mob violence and will do so at any time, well knowing they will not be called to account for so doing. I repeat, Governor, that if this man is reinstated, it will simply mean an increase of lynchings in the state of Illinois and an encouragement to mob violence."

By the time she finished, it was late afternoon. Her speech had been so stirring that when she sat down, a number of her opponents came over to shake her hand and say how well she had done. Even Sheriff Davis shook her hand and said, "I bear you no grudge for what you have done, Mrs. Barnett." But probably neither Davis nor any of his supporters thought there was the slightest chance of the governor's ruling against him.

Wells-Barnett returned to Chicago and waited. A few days after the hearing Governor Deneen issued his verdict. It shocked much of the nation: Frank Davis would not be reinstated because he had not protected his prisoner properly. "Mob violence has no place in Illinois," the governor declared. This decision not only helped put an end to lynchings in Illinois, it marked one of the first times that a person who went along with a lynching was punished.

Shortly after the governor's decision, the *Chicago Defender* published an article about the landmark ruling, proclaiming: "If we only had a few men with the backbone of Mrs. Barnett, lynching would soon come to a halt in America."

But until she told the story in her autobiography many years later, no one outside the Barnett family realized that, if not for thirteen-year-old Charles, she might never have gone to Springfield to argue the case.

"Reaching the Boys and Men Who Were Farthest Down and Out"

WHEN ALFREDA WAS BORN in 1904, Ida B. Wells-Barnett was forty-two years old—an age when most women of her era were becoming grandmothers, not mothers. Just as she gave birth at a relatively late age, she also began a series of new projects during her forties and fifties to go along with her anti-lynching crusade.

Wells-Barnett believed in the saying "There is strength in numbers." Since forming the Ida B. Wells Club, she had been involved in establishing many civil rights organizations, a list of which might fill a page of this book. Most of these groups have disappeared or merged with other organizations. However, in 1909 she helped start a civil rights organization that is still going strong. Because of her militant reputation, she played an odd role in the formation of this organization, the National Association for the Advancement of Colored People (NAACP).

The year 1909 marked the one hundredth anniversary of the birth of Abraham Lincoln, who had done the most of any president to end slavery. A group of people, both black and white, thought there was no better way to celebrate the anniversary than to form a civil rights group that would put an end to such evils as segregation and lynching.

By this time black leaders had become even more sharply divided

Mrs. Florence Kelley, 105 E. 22 St., New York, N.Y.;
Mr. Paul Kennaday, 640 Madison Avenue, New York, N.Y.;
Mrs. Frances R. Keyser, 217 E. 86 St., New York, N.Y.;
Mrs. Mary D. McLean, 259 W. 92 St., New York, N.Y.;
Rev. A. Clayton Powell, 255 W. 134 St., New York, N.Y.;
Mr. Charles Edward Russell, Hotel Broztell, New York, N.Y.;
Prof. Joel E. Spingarn, 9 W. 73 St., New York, N.Y.;
Miss Lillian D. Wald, 265 Henry St., New York, N.Y.;
Mr. William English Walling, Hotel Brevoort, New York, N.Y.;
Dr. Owen M. Waller, 762 Herkimer St., Brooklyn, N.Y.;
Mr. W.I. Bulkley, Ridgefield Park, N.J.;
Mr. Albert E. Pillsbury, 6 Beacon St., Boston, Mass.;
Miss Jane Addams, Hull House, Chicago, Ill.;
Mrs. Ida B. Wells Barnett, 3235 Rhodes Ave., Chicago, Ill.;
Dr. Charles E. Bentley, 100 State St., Chicago, Ill.;
Dr. Noah F. Mossell, 143 Lombard St., Philadelphia, Pa.;
Dr. William A. Sinclair, 1221 Pine St., Philadelphia, Pa.;
Mrs. Mary Church Terrell, 326 T St., N.W., Washington, D.C.;
Rev. J. Milton Waldron, 1334 V St., Washington, D.C.;

The annual meeting of the corporation shall be held on the first Monday of January in each year.

IN TESTIMONY WHEREOF, we have made and signed this certificate in duplicate and have hereunto set our hands and affixed our respective seals this 25th day of May, 1911.

3 W.E.B. DuBois _____ (L.S.)

1 John Haynes Holmes _____ (L.S.)

2 Oswald Garrison Villard _____ (L.S.)

4 Walter E. Sachs _____ (L.S.)

5 Mary White Ovington _____ (L.S.)

Some names of the organizers of the NAACP

between the radicals and the Bookerites. W. E. B. Du Bois had replaced Wells-Barnett as the leading voice of the radicals. The first black person granted a doctoral degree by Harvard University, Du Bois taught history and economics at Atlanta University and was the author of *The Souls of Black Folk,* a landmark book of essays about being black in America. Black radicals had turned away from Wells-Barnett because even *they* considered her too militant. She had clashed with many people who compromised on civil rights issues, from Frances E. Willard to President William McKinley. In *Mob Rule in New Orleans* she had confronted white people by demanding, "Men and women of America, are you proud of this record [of lynching] which the [white] race has made for itself?" Wells-Barnett was resented for another reason. Most black activisits were men, and like other men of the time, they did not want to be led by a woman.

On February 12—Abraham Lincoln's birthday—Ida attended a meeting in Chicago's Orchestra Hall at which plans were made for founding the NAACP. That same day a petition calling for the formation of the new organization was issued by sixty prominent people from around the country, including Ida B. Wells-Barnett. The signers of this petition, which is known as "the Call," are considered the founders of the NAACP. However, Wells-Barnett never took an active role in the NAACP, which she regarded as a timid organization geared toward wealthy rather than poor and powerless black people. Interestingly, in 1966, fifty-seven years after its founding, the NAACP denounced the Black Power movement, which had just begun. Had she still been alive, Wells-Barnett probably would have embraced Black Power, which advised black people to demand, not request, justice.

Meanwhile, thousands of black southerners were moving to Chicago and other northern cities in the early 1900s in search of a better life. They didn't always find the opportunities they had expected, and some who wound up in the streets ran afoul of the law. Ida often visited young prison inmates who told her how their inability to find work had led to their troubles. In 1910 she decided to do something about "reaching the boys and men who were farthest down and out." She decided to open a neighborhood center, similar to Jane Addams's Hull House, for black Chicagoans. A wealthy white newspaper publisher and his wife pledged to pay the costs for a year if she found a location for her center.

Wells-Barnett found an empty building at 2830 South State Street. There, on May 1, 1910, she opened the Negro Fellowship League Reading Room and Social Center. Upstairs was a dormitory where homeless men could sleep. Downstairs were rooms for music, games, and reading. The reading room was stocked with Chicago newspapers, so that

The Fellowship Herald

THE FELLOWSHIP HERALD CO
PUBLISHERS.

Ida B. Wells-Barnett, Editor.

Issued Weekly by
Fellowship Herald Publishing &
Printing Company.

FOUNDED MAY 7th, 1911.

Subscription Rates in Advance
$1.50 per year.
Advertising Rates, $1.25 per agate in.

OFFICE: 2830 STATE STREET

WANTED—MEN!

God give us men! A time like this
demands.

Strong minds, great hearts, true
faith and ready hands;

Men whom the lust of office does
not kill;

Men whom the spoils of office cannot buy;

Men who possess opinions and a
will;

Men who have honor, men who will
not lie;

Men who can stand before a dema-
gogue,

And damn his treacherous flatteries
without winking!

Tall men, sun crowned who live
above the fog;

In public duty, and in private
thinking;

For while the rabble with their
thumb worn creeds,

Their large professions and their
little deeds

Mingle in selfish strife, lo freedom
weeps,

Wrong rules the land and waiting
justice sleeps.

three little Negro boys. Surely if the
religion of the Lord Jesus Christ is
needed anywhere it is needed in this
district. Elsewhere in this paper will
be found the account of a minister in
Detroit who has decided to preach
from the curb to the people who con-
gregate there. Perhaps if our ministers here would do this, they could
preach some of these men off the
street corners and out of the dens in
the churches

A Move in the Right Direction.

Rev. R. L. Bradbury has announced
that he will give a short open air address to the boys who neglect to attend church, at the corner of St.
Antoine and Brewster sts., Sunday,
June 11, at 3 o'clock in the afternoon.
This is an excellent move in the right
direction and may be emulated with
profit by the ministers of the city.

There are many spots farther down
town where the inhabitants would be
greatly benefitted by a series of good
common sense lectures and it is hoped
this work will be pushed.

If the habitues of the underworld
even, find that the ministry has an interest in their temporal as well as
their spiritual welfare it cannot help
but make better men and women of
them and greatly lessen the tendency
to a wretched criminal career.—The
Detroit Informer.

Watch for the Woman's Edition of
The Fellowship Herald. It will be
out soon and will be an eight or
twelve page edition, and will give
news, information and write ups of
the prominent race women and their
work as individuals as club women, as
church workers, as wives, mothers,
sisters and daughters. Subscribe now
so you may be sure of getting One

A rare copy of Ida's Fellowship Herald

the men could comb the job ads, and also with southern papers, so that they could read about events back home. Members of the Sunday school class she taught volunteered to help at the center, and Ida herself worked there several hours each day. From seven-thirty in the morning until nine at night, the center's Employment Bureau helped job seekers find work. In addition Wells-Barnett organized a Fellowship Chorus that performed at eight-thirty on Tuesday evenings for anyone who came in to listen. A Boys' Club offered games and other activities for neighborhood youths at seven-thirty on Friday nights. Besides all this she published a newspaper, the *Fellowship Herald,* which described the center's work and contemporary civil rights issues.

Between 1896 and 1911 Ferdinand Barnett was assistant state's attorney for Cook County, in which Chicago is located. In that capacity he encountered many men entangled in legal troubles and met numerous judges and police officers. Ferdinand and his legal colleagues directed many young men to the center, where his wife helped them find jobs. Through the center Ida also became involved in several prominent lynching and civil rights cases.

Soon after the center opened, Ida learned of a young man who had tried to kill himself in a Chicago jail cell by eating ground glass. She looked into the incident and uncovered some distressing facts. The young man, Steve Green, was from Arkansas. Hoping to improve his life, he had attempted to move off the plantation where he was employed. The plantation owner had tried to prevent his leaving, becoming so enraged that he shot and wounded Green. Steve Green defended himself, killing his attacker. Certain that he would be lynched for killing a white man if he remained in Arkansas, Green fled to Chicago, but authorities back home learned of his whereabouts and arranged for his return. Steve Green's unsuccessful suicide attempt had occurred just before he was to be sent back to Arkansas.

By the time Wells-Barnett learned all this, a deputy sheriff from Arkansas had come for Green and was taking him home by train. As they traveled south through Illinois, the deputy told Green, "Steve, by this time tomorrow you will be the most popular man in Arkansas, for a thousand men will be waiting to burn you alive for killing your employer."

While Green was being taken south, Wells-Barnett contacted Illinois authorities, who said she could return Green to Chicago—if she could apprehend him before he left the state. She arranged for a hundred-dollar reward to be given to any Illinois sheriff who arrested Green and took him back to Chicago. Green was not located until he had reached the southernmost tip of Illinois—Alexander County, where Wells-Barnett had recently gotten Sheriff Frank Davis removed. Just as the train was about to be ferried across the Mississippi River out of Illinois, either the new Alexander County sheriff or a deputy found Green in one of the train cars. He placed his hand on Green's shoulder and informed the Arkansas deputy, "I arrest this man in the name of the great state of Illinois."

Never was anyone happier about being arrested! Instead of being lynched in Arkansas, Green was taken back to Chicago. He apparently was hidden at Wells-Barnett's Negro Fellowship League center while the states of Arkansas and Illinois argued over him. Finally it became clear that Illinois Governor Charles S. Deneen had no choice but to send him back to Arkansas.

Wells-Barnett refused to send Steve Green back to almost certain death. She decided that there was a higher law than the one that said Green must be returned to Arkansas. Steve Green suddenly vanished. Later it was learned that Ida helped him escape to Canada. Eventually the Arkansas authorities gave up trying to arrest him, and Green was able to return to Chicago. Wells-Barnett welcomed him at her center and helped him find a job.

Another case she learned about through the center concerned a man facing a "legal" lynching. Joe Campbell was an inmate at the penitentiary at Joliet, Illinois. A model prisoner, he was made a "trusty," meaning that he was deemed sufficiently trustworthy to have special privileges. But when a fire broke out in the warden's quarters, killing the warden's wife, Joe Campbell was blamed. Reports from the penitentiary said that he had confessed to the crime and would be executed.

On the evening that she learned about the Joe Campbell case, Wells-Barnett sat down to dinner but showed no interest in her food. Questioned by her family, she told them about Campbell. "When I think of that poor devil being persecuted down there in the penitentiary, the reports assuming he is guilty without giving him a chance to defend himself, I can't eat." She excused herself from the table and went upstairs to lie in bed and think. It didn't take her long to decide to do all she could to help Joe Campbell.

Ida visited Campbell in prison and learned that he had been tortured to make him confess. Furthermore, the warden's wife had been about to ask the board of pardons to release Campbell, so why would he kill her? Ida wrote newspaper articles supporting Campbell and convinced her husband to take the case. Ferdinand spent six weeks in Joliet gathering facts and arguing Campbell's case in court. Eventually Ferdinand brought Joe Campbell's case before the Illinois Supreme Court. Although they were unable to win his release, Ida and Ferdinand at least managed to save Joe Campbell's life. Through the couple's efforts, his death sentence was reduced to life in prison.

At the end of its first year the Negro Fellowship League was clearly a success. About 45 people were staying there each night. Ida and her staff had found jobs for 115 young men. The newspaper publisher and his wife who had provided the funding were so pleased with the results that they supported the center for another two years. But at the end of that time they informed Wells-Barnett that they had spent upward of $9,000 on the project and could not continue to fund it. Since the rent on the building was $175 a month—far beyond her means—it appeared that Wells-Barnett would have to close the center.

Ida refused to give in to what seemed inevitable. First she moved the center to smaller quarters two blocks to the south, at 3005 South State Street. The new building was just a storefront, with a rent of only $35 a month, but since even that was too expensive for her, she decided to find herself a paying job. She was hired as Chicago's first female probation officer, supervising convicted criminals whom the courts allowed to remain free as long as they maintained good behavior. The job paid $150 a month and required her to be on duty in court from nine in the morning until five in the afternoon. While it was very demanding, the job meshed perfectly with her Negro Fellowship League activities. In the evenings she went to her center, where she generally worked to nine or ten at night. She told many of her probationers to report to her at the center, so that she could keep her eye on them while helping them find work.

Wells-Barnett often said that many young men landed in trouble because "only one social center welcomes the Negro, and that is the saloon." Although not as segregated as the South, northern cities had stores, theaters, and public places where blacks were not welcome. Shortly before she began the Negro Fellowship League, Wells-Barnett helped establish a theater where black people could be entertained by black actors and musicians. She invited a hundred women to a benefit at which she collected money to help fund Chicago's Pekin Theater, which was located near her Negro Fellowship League. Their work in the Pekin Theater helped many budding actors and musicians, including Charles Gilpin, who later achieved fame acting in such plays as John Drinkwater's *Abraham Lincoln* and Eugene O'Neill's *The Emperor Jones*.

Meanwhile, Wells-Barnett had become convinced that Susan B. Anthony was right after all: Things might improve when women won the vote. On January 30, 1913, she founded the Alpha Suffrage Club, Illinois's first voting rights organization for black women. It met at the Negro Fellowship League Reading Room and Social Center every Wednesday night at eight-thirty. Soon after the Alpha Suffrage Club was founded, its members and their daughters marched in a big suffrage parade in downtown Chicago. Wearing a white dress with a white banner across it saying ALPHA SUFFRAGE, eight-year-old Alfreda marched down Michigan Avenue next to her mother.

Wells-Barnett began a newsletter for the organization, the *Alpha Suffrage Record*. Now fifty years old, she was editing two newspapers (the *Fellowship Herald* was the other), running the Negro Fellowship League and the Alpha Suffrage Club, holding a full-time job as a probation officer, attending a variety of civil rights meetings, and producing a barrage of newspaper articles about lynching and segregation.

Among other things, the Alpha Suffrage Club worked on behalf of Oscar DePriest, who became Chicago's first black alderman in 1915. In 1928 DePriest was elected from Illinois to the U.S. House of Representatives, thus becoming the first African American to serve in the House since George H. White's retirement from Congress in 1901.

In early 1913, just before Woodrow Wilson's inauguration as the twenty-eighth president, five thousand women from around the country met in Washington, D.C., to demand the vote. Ida B. Wells-Barnett

The women's suffrage parade in Washington, D.C., in 1913

traveled to the nation's capital to march in the huge suffrage parade. However, the leaders of the national suffrage movement asked her to march in a separate colored section rather than with the Illinois delegation. When she asked why, she was told that her presence would annoy southern white women.

"No!" Wells-Barnett informed the leaders, she would not march in a segregated colored section. She would march with the white Illinois suffragists, and let the southerners be damned if they didn't like it! Soon after the event Bettiola H. Fortson composed a poem titled "Queen of Our Race" commemorating Ida B. Wells-Barnett's march near the White House:

> Side by side with the whites she walked,
> Step after step the southerners balked,
> But Illinois, fond of order and grace,
> Stuck to the black Queen of our race.
>
> 'Tis true, they're able at this age to bar,
> But justice will soon send the doors ajar
> And sit the black and white face to face.
> There will be seen the Queen of our race.
>
> Page after page in history you'll read
> Of one who was ready and able to lead,
> Who set the nation on fire with her pace
> And the Heroine will be the Queen of our race.

Eight months later Wells-Barnett returned to Washington, D.C.—this time to go *inside* the White House. It was not a social call. President Wilson had disappointed black Americans in many ways. For one thing, several members of his cabinet had forbidden their black secretaries and clerks to use the same restaurants and bathrooms as their white employees. Black people wondered: Could the country ever be desegregated if the president allowed his highest-level advisers to practice discrimination?

William Monroe Trotter, the fiery editor of the *Boston Guardian,* had formed the National Equal Rights League to fight such injustices. Ida joined the organization and was asked to accompany her friend Trotter to the White House to discuss the problem with President Wilson.

Wells-Barnett told Wilson that his cabinet members were segregating employees by race, and insisted it was his duty as president to end the practice. Trotter showed the president a printed order from a department head forbidding black and white clerks to use the same bathrooms and restaurants. Wilson said he doubted that segregation was occurring, but that he would investigate. A year passed and the president did nothing, so Trotter made another appointment to speak to him. Wells-

William Monroe Trotter

Barnett did not accompany Trotter this time, explaining that "it was not convenient" for her to leave Chicago just then. Few people would pass up an opportunity to meet with the president, and we can only speculate as to her reasons for doing so. One possibility is that she had pressing business at her Negro Fellowship League and placed the welfare of "the boys and men who were farthest down and out" ahead of a meeting with the president of the United States.

The meeting did not go well without her. President Wilson said that he had discovered that "the segregation was caused by friction between colored and white clerks." Furthermore, the president told Trotter that segregation was "not humiliating but a benefit" for African Americans. Trotter became so enraged that the White House security force escorted him out of the president's home.

Wilson was still president when the United States entered what was then called the Great War on April 6, 1917. That August black soldiers in Houston, Texas, having endured racial insults to the breaking point, killed sixteen white citizens, including five police officers. Responding to demands by southern whites, the army took harsh revenge. To this day accounts of what occurred afterward vary widely. A number of black soldiers—some say as many as thirteen, others as few as six—were found guilty of the murders and hanged. Their bodies were thrown into unmarked graves. Dozens more were sentenced to life in prison.

Wells-Barnett felt that the government had perpetrated a "legal" lynching and had inflicted a much more severe punishment than would have been the case had the soldiers been white and the victims black. She decided to hold a memorial service for the hanged soldiers. But when she called the pastor of a large black Chicago church and asked if she could use the building for the service, the answer was no. She received similar responses when she called several more churches.

The pastors were afraid. During the Great War numerous "citizens' organizations" were formed to make sure that Americans were sufficiently

President Woodrow Wilson

"patriotic." Because the United States was fighting Germany, Americans of German heritage were widely persecuted. They were fired from their jobs and insulted by their neighbors, and their German-language books were burned—despite the fact that thousands of German Americans fought for the United States. If white Americans were persecuting each other, African Americans knew that they could expect trouble unless they demonstrated their loyalty to the government. A black church that protested the execution of the soldiers in the Houston incident could be burned down by the self-appointed guardians of patriotism.

In anticipation of the service, Wells-Barnett had ordered hundreds of buttons bearing the inscription IN MEMORIAL MARTYRED NEGRO

SOLDIERS. Unable to hold the memorial, she decided at least to pass out the buttons. She had just begun distributing them to everyone who was interested when a newspaper reporter visited her at the Negro Fellowship League and asked to see a button. Ida gave it to him, hoping he would write a story sympathetic to the executed soldiers. Instead he hurried back to his office and made a phone call.

Less than two hours later two tough-looking white men arrived at the Negro Fellowship League. They identified themselves as agents with the U.S. Secret Service and issued a warning. If Wells-Barnett continued to distribute the buttons, she could expect to be arrested.

"On what charge?" Wells-Barnett asked.

"Why, for treason!" answered one of the agents.

Treason means aiding the enemy in wartime, an extremely serious crime that could be punished by life in prison or even by a death sentence. What with the power of the U.S. government behind them, their threat that she might be charged with treason, and the fact that they were two white men confronting one black woman, the agents expected that Wells-Barnett would quickly hand over the buttons. They received the shock of their lives.

"Treason!" she replied. "I understand treason to mean giving aid and comfort to the enemy in time of war. How can the distribution of this little button do that?"

"Well," said the other agent, "we can't arrest you, Mrs. Barnett, but we can confiscate your buttons. Will you give us the buttons?"

"No!" she said firmly.

"Why," he said, astonished by her boldness, "you have criticized the government!"

"Yes, and the government deserves to be criticized. I think it was a dastardly thing to hang those men as if they were criminals and put them in holes in the ground just as if they had been dead dogs. If it is treason for me to think and say so, then make the most of it. I'd rather go down in history as one lone Negro who dared to tell the government that it had done a dastardly thing than to save my skin by taking back what I have said. I would consider it an honor to spend whatever years are necessary in prison."

The Secret Service agents stared at her in amazement. They departed without the buttons, and she was never again threatened about distributing them. She wore one of the buttons herself for many years following this incident.

Despite what had occurred, Wells-Barnett joined the war effort. Four hundred thousand African American troops served in the Great War—in all-black units. They included Ida's stepson, Ferdinand Barnett Jr. Many black soldiers were stationed at Camp Grant near Rockford, Illinois, eighty miles northwest of Chicago, before being sent off to war. As Christmas of 1917 approached, local patriotic groups provided white soldiers at army camps with gifts, but the black soldiers at Camp Grant, many of whom had come from the South, were generally ignored. A white army general invited Wells-Barnett to Camp Grant and asked: Could she arrange for some Christmas cheer for twelve hundred black soldiers?

Ida held fundraisers and collected enough money to buy a half-pound box of candy and several other gifts for each of those twelve hundred "soldier boys," as she called them. She also arranged to post a man at the Chicago train station to welcome newly arriving black soldiers, many of whom had never been away from home before.

The United States and its allies won the war in November 1918, and a peace conference was scheduled for the following January in Paris, France. Everyone hoped the conference would establish a lasting peace and create a better life for all the world's people. Ida B. Wells-Barnett felt that African Americans should send representatives to the conference to propose that a "racial equality clause" be part of the peace agreement. She contacted William Monroe Trotter and arranged for the 1918 convention of his National Equal Rights League to be held in Chicago. Trotter and his supporters decided that he, Wells-Barnett, and

Ida wearing her IN MEMORIAL MARTYRED NEGRO SOLDIERS *button*

nine other people should attend the Paris conference. However, President Wilson wouldn't allow them to attend, and the government denied them the passports required for overseas travel. Of the eleven intended delegates only Trotter went overseas, crossing the ocean by disguising himself as a ship's cook. Once he reached France, Trotter was totally ignored.

The peace conference was not effective. Germany, which had been defeated, was forced to sign a treaty it found objectionable. Many people believe that this was a contributing factor to the deadliest war in history. Instead of being "the war to end all wars," as people had hoped, the Great War became known as World War I. An even bloodier conflict, World War II, began just over twenty years later. Would Ida B. Wells-Barnett's presence at the peace conference have made any difference? This is one of those intriguing might-have-beens of history, but of course we can never know the answer.

Barnett family portrait from 1917. Top row, from left: Hulette (Albert's wife), Herman, Sergeant Ferdinand Jr. (who served in World War I), Ida Jr., Charles, Albert; front row, from left: Hulette Jr., Ferdinand Sr., Beatrice, Audrey, Florence (in front of Ida), Ida B. Wells-Barnett, Alfreda (holding her mother's hand). Hulette Jr., Beatrice, Audrey, and Florence were Albert and Hulette Barnett's daughters.

The Tide of Hatred

AFTER WORKING AS a probation officer for three years, Wells-Barnett lost her job. It was a matter of politics. In Chicago's mayoral election of 1915 she supported the judge who had appointed her as a probation officer. He was defeated, and six months later the new administration replaced her with one of its own people.

Still, she managed to keep the Negro Fellowship League open for a few more years. People donated money to help her pay the rent for the State Street storefront, and she and Ferdinand probably dipped into their own funds to keep the center running. Ferdinand was now earning a good living as a lawyer—so good that in 1919 the family moved to a large home at 3624 Grand Boulevard, now known as Martin Luther King Drive. The house featured a third-floor ballroom that Ida converted into an apartment for her son Herman and his bride.

But Ida and Ferdinand couldn't continue to funnel their savings into the Negro Fellowship League. Just after Thanksgiving of 1920 she closed the center permanently and turned the keys over to the landlord of the building. She had run the Negro Fellowship League for ten years. During that time she had helped find jobs for approximately a thousand men, and had provided a place to stay for many others who might have otherwise been left to roam the streets.

She still wrote about lynching, but less often than before. Although the problem had not been conquered, the situation had improved. The death toll was dropping steadily: sixty-nine lynchings in 1915, fifty-four in 1916, thirty-eight in 1917. Sadly, by then another kind of racial conflict was claiming many lives.

As large numbers of black southerners moved into northern cities, what Ida called the tide of hatred became as big a problem in the North as it was in the South. Social scientists explained that this was because whites felt threatened when African Americans competed with them for jobs and housing. The Ku Klux Klan, which had been rather quiet for a number of years, had reorganized in 1915. The new Klan recruited members in both the South and the North, and within a few years boasted a membership of four million people.

The spread of racism resulted in numerous race riots throughout the nation. Often a single incident—a quarrel between black and white teenagers or an attack on a black youth who entered a white neighborhood—sparked fighting that turned some cities into war zones. As with lynchings, black people suffered the most. The police usually sided with the whites, and courts tended to blame the blacks for starting the riots.

On July 2, 1917, one of the deadliest race riots in U.S. history occurred in East St. Louis, Illinois, across the Mississippi River from St. Louis, Missouri. White mobs attacked East St. Louis's black neighborhoods, setting fires and shooting at residents. Estimates of the number of black people killed in this riot ranged from forty to two hundred. An exact body count was impossible because the destruction was so widespread and because thousands of black people driven out of their neighborhoods never returned. To this day East St. Louis feels the effects of this riot, which was actually more like a massacre. The day before the riot the city's population had been 77,500. So many people fled the city that three years later, in 1920, its population had dropped to 67,000. The decline continued, and by 1998 only 37,000 people lived in East St. Louis, Illinois.

Black Chicagoans felt that their city, as the largest in Illinois, should send a protest to Governor Frank O. Lowden about the East St. Louis slaughter. Ida B. Wells-Barnett was chosen to present this protest, and funds were raised to send her downstate.

She took the train to East St. Louis, arriving there at seven o'clock on the morning of July 5, three days after the riot. As the fifty-five-year-old civil rights leader prepared to leave the train, the conductor told her that it was too dangerous for her to enter the city, and that she should go on to St. Louis instead. "Get back on that train!" he told her.

"This is the station where I want to get off," she said, stepping down. The conductor shrugged and climbed back onto the train, which soon pulled out of the station.

Looking around, she saw that she was the only person to have left the train at East St. Louis. The only other person on the platform was a National Guardsman, who stood holding his gun. When she asked about the conditions in town, the guardsman answered, "Bad!" The violence hadn't ended, and it was dangerous for a lone black woman to walk through the city.

Acting as though nothing was wrong, she walked up the main street to the city hall, where the National Guard was headquartered. At first the only black person she could find was the city hall janitor. He explained that the town's other black people had been killed, had fled, or were in hiding.

She spent a day gathering information in East St. Louis and across the river in St. Louis, where many of the black people had sought refuge. At times during that day she was threatened with arrest and forced to ride in a police wagon. Everyone she met told a slightly different story, but she finally pieced together what she believed were the facts.

White people had become angry that African Americans were rapidly being hired in the area's industrial plants. Sensing that an attack by white mobs might be coming, several leaders of East St. Louis's black community had visited Governor Lowden a month earlier. They had implored him to do all in his power to prevent trouble. When the governor ignored their request, some members of the black community armed themselves in case they had to defend their families. They agreed to ring a church bell, as the colonists had done during the war for American independence, to signal that they were under attack.

On Sunday evening, July 1, a large car filled with white men drove through a black neighborhood. The men shot into homes of black residents, then sped off. The church bell was rung, and when the car returned and the white men again fired their guns, some black men returned the fire. Allegedly two men in the car who were law officers were killed. Word spread among the white townspeople that two law officers, innocently driving through a black neighborhood, had been shot to death. Mobs formed, roaming through black neighborhoods burning and shooting. The National Guard was called out, but instead of protecting the black people in town, they stood by and watched the massacre. As best Wells-Barnett could determine, more than 150 black people had been killed.

Armed with these facts, Wells-Barnett returned to Chicago, then went off to Springfield to present her report to the governor. Lowden paid little attention to her, for he had been told that she was a radical, and, besides, white leaders planned to blame the black people of East St. Louis for their own massacre.

Sixty-five white people were convicted of taking part in the riot. However, most of them spent a short time in jail—in many cases only a few days. Only ten of them were sentenced to as long as five years in prison. On the other hand, fifteen black men charged with provoking the riot were each sentenced to fifteen years in prison. Another black man, Dr. LeRoy Bundy, was charged with obtaining the guns and ammunition with which his neighbors had tried to protect themselves. Word went out that Illinois authorities from the governor on down were intent on making an example of Dr. Bundy, who was sentenced to life imprisonment. Since the black townspeople had acted in self-defense and had suffered nearly all the deaths in the riot, Ida B. Wells-Barnett considered this a clear miscarriage of justice.

Robert S. Abbott, owner and publisher of the influential black newspaper the *Chicago Defender,* asked Wells-Barnett to investigate and write about Dr. Bundy. She traveled to Belleville, Illinois, a few miles from East St. Louis, where he was imprisoned, and met with him. Ida found him to be an unlikely troublemaker—a prominent dentist and auto dealer whose success was resented by many white people. She wrote articles about Dr. Bundy in the *Defender* and arranged for Ferdinand to assist in his case. Thanks partly to the efforts of Ida and Ferdinand, Dr. Bundy was released on bail. He was eventually acquitted of the charges by the Illinois Supreme Court, and he moved to Cleveland, where he resumed his dental practice. Ida also worked for the release of the other fifteen men, helping them win a pardon from Illinois Governor Len Small after they had served ten of their fifteen years in prison.

By the end of World War I the mood in black communities had changed. Before, when white ruffians had beaten or murdered their people, African Americans had locked themselves in their homes, hoping to avoid further trouble. When whites had warned them not to apply for certain jobs or move into their neighborhoods, black people had generally obeyed them. But thousands of African Americans who had bravely served their country in the war felt that they had a right to live and work where they chose and to protect their families from violence. Besides, the military had taught them how to fight. When attacked, they now fought back, as Dr. Bundy and his friends had done. The growing trend of blacks defending themselves—and of whites resenting blacks who demanded their rights—contributed to a rash of riots after the war ended. So much blood was shed in the hot months of 1919 that author James Weldon Johnson, composer of the African American national anthem "Lift Every Voice and Sing," called this period the Red Summer. Twenty-five race riots occurred across the United States that year, causing dozens of deaths and thousands of injuries. Race riots in Washington, D.C., resulted in the deaths of six people and injury to one hundred fifty others. Major riots also occurred in Phillips

Chicago race riot of 1919

County, Arkansas, and in Longview, Texas. In addition there was a terrible riot in Chicago during the Red Summer.

In 1919 the Barnetts moved into their large home on Grand Boulevard. Other black families also moved into what had been all-white parts of Chicago. White homeowners vowed to halt what they called the Negro invasion of their neighborhoods. A series of bombings of black homes took place on and near Grand Boulevard. Sensing a disaster in the making, Wells-Barnett wrote a letter that appeared in the *Chicago Tribune.* "It looks very much like Chicago is trying to rival the South in its race hatred against the Negro," she said. "Especially does this seem so when we consider the bombing of Negro homes and the indifference of the public to these outrages." City officials must "set the wheels of justice in motion," she added, "before it is too late and Chicago be disgraced by the bloody outrages that have disgraced East St. Louis."

City officials did not heed her warning. Three weeks later the disaster she had predicted occurred. It began at a Lake Michigan beach on July 27. On that Sunday a group of black boys swimming near the Twenty-sixth Street beach drifted several hundred yards south to the Twenty-ninth Street beach—beyond the customary boundary separating the races. A white man hurled rocks at the boys, striking one of them in the head. The boy sank into the water and drowned. Policemen at the scene refused to arrest the ruffian who had caused the boy's death. News and rumors of the drowning spread. Soon groups of whites and blacks were throwing rocks at one another. Shots were fired. The fighting spread to other areas of the city and turned into a race war.

For five days white and black mobs roamed the city, beating and killing people and setting fires. Like most other Chicagoans, Ferdinand and the children stayed indoors. But Ida walked through burned-out neighborhoods, gathering information in order to make a report to authorities. The riot took a terrible toll. Twenty-three African Americans and fifteen white people were killed. The official list of injured persons stood at 537, although there were probably hundreds more who didn't report their wounds. A thousand houses had been burned, leaving thousands of Chicagoans homeless.

Wells-Barnett submitted her report to Chicago officials, but little was done to punish the offenders or to "stem the tide of race hatred," as she expressed it. Had these same officials listened to her three weeks earlier, perhaps the worst race riot in Chicago history would have been averted.

"Eternal Vigilance Is the Price of Liberty"

O NE WEEK AFTER CLOSING the Negro Fellowship League in late 1920, Ida became ill and was taken to the hospital. On December 15 she was operated on for gallstones. Complications occurred, and it appeared that she might not survive. Finally, after five weeks, she was well enough to leave the hospital, but after going home, she suffered a relapse and remained bedridden for an additional eight weeks. It took her an entire year to recover.

"During that year," she later wrote, "I did more serious thinking from a personal point of view than ever before in my life." She had much to be proud of. First there was her family. In 1921 her stepsons, Ferdinand Jr. and Albert, were thirty-seven and thirty-five years old, and her own children, Charles, Herman, Ida, and Alfreda, ranged in age from twenty-five to seventeen. She often referred to Herman as her problem child, because he gambled and had to be helped out of trouble by his parents, but he and the other children all eventually became successful.

Ferdinand Jr. graduated from what is now the Illinois Institute of Technology, while Albert attended law school and became the city editor for the *Chicago Defender*. Charles, Ida's first-born, had his mother's temper. At Chicago's Wendell Phillips High School he had an argument with a teacher that resulted in his quitting school. He left home and for a time worked as a chauffeur in Milwaukee, Wisconsin. Later he established his own printing business. Herman became a lawyer and worked as his father's associate in Chicago's Barnett & Barnett law firm. He then moved to California and worked in the State Employment Service. Young Ida was her father's secretary for many years. Alfreda graduated from the University of Chicago at the early age of nineteen and became active in civic organizations, following in her mother's footsteps.

Ida Sr. was also winning her long struggle against lynching. The number of people killed in lynchings dropped to thirty-three in 1923 and sixteen in 1924. And although there were more race riots, during Wells-Barnett's lifetime there was never another period as bad as the Red Summer of 1919.

Ida didn't travel much anymore, for her operation in 1920 had sapped the remarkable reservoir of energy of her younger years. Nonetheless, in 1922, at the invitation of one of the prisoners, she went down to Little Rock, Arkansas, to speak to the twelve men condemned after the

White people about to move against blacks in the Phillips County (Arkansas) riot

Aftermath of the Tulsa, Oklahoma, race riot of 1921

Phillips County riot. Freeing those men, which her pamphlet *The Arkansas Race Riot* helped accomplish, was one of her proudest achievements.

Despite the steady improvements, Wells-Barnett thought that civil rights progress was occurring too slowly and that black people shouldn't be satisfied with small victories such as the "first black alderman" or the "first black congressman." Accusing the younger generation of being "do-nothings," she reentered club work to stir things up. In about 1923—nearly thirty years after she had resigned following Herman's birth—she was once again elected president of the Ida B. Wells Club. At the 1924 convention of the National Association of Colored Women, held in Chicago, she ran for president of the organization against Mary McLeod Bethune. She had antagonized many of the group's leaders by referring to them as do-nothings, however, and lost the election.

One day in 1927 or 1928 Wells-Barnett was approached by a young woman with a question. She had been the only black person at a Young Women's Christian Association religious service where each person was asked to name a real-life heroine. When her turn came she said,

"Ida B. Wells-Barnett," only she couldn't explain what Wells-Barnett had done beyond a general idea that it involved lynching.

"Mrs. Barnett," said the young woman, "won't you please tell me what it was you did, so the next time I am asked such a question I can give an intelligent answer?"

Ida asked the woman how old she was and was told twenty-five. Suddenly Ida realized that most of her anti-lynching work had taken place in the 1890s and early 1900s, before the current generation had been born. As lynching was conquered, the new generation cared less and less about the struggle to end it. Wells-Barnett decided to answer the young woman's question in an unusual way. She would write her autobiography, chronicling her life and the major events in her crusade against lynching. She began the project in 1928, opening with the story of the young woman asking her who she was.

Wells-Barnett dedicated the book to "our youth [who are] entitled to the facts of race history which only the participants can give." She wrote in a simple, straightforward style—as though she were speaking to the young woman and other members of her generation. Almost every day she wrote and revised her manuscript, until it was one hundred, two hundred, then three hundred pages long; and still it continued to grow. Herman, who for a time worked as his mother's secretary, typed the manuscript for her.

Ida had one more surprise for her friends and family. In 1920 the United States at long last had granted women their voting rights—fourteen years after the death of Susan B. Anthony and one hundred years after Anthony's birth. Around the country small numbers of women began to run for public office. By 1930 there were several black male representatives in the Illinois state legislature, but Wells-Barnett didn't think they were doing enough to combat segregation, joblessness, and hunger. She decided to enter the 1930 election for the Illinois state senate. Although she was approaching her sixty-eighth birthday, she threw herself wholeheartedly into the campaign. Traveling about her district,

Black people lined up to register for voting

she often delivered two speeches a day. Ferdinand assisted her, and together they placed six hundred posters in windows of stores and residences. They also distributed ten thousand cards, ten thousand letters, and twenty thousand newsletters.

Wells-Barnett ran as an independent candidate, while her opponents had the support of powerful political organizations. She finished far behind the winner, polling 585 votes to his 6,604. Still, she made history as one of the first black women in the nation to run for public office. In retrospect her pioneering effort can be viewed as a victory, for in running for the Illinois state senate against great odds, she paved the way for other women—white and black—to make successful bids for elected office in more recent times.

In 1930 Ferdinand was seventy-eight years old and Ida was sixty-eight. With Ferdinand nearing retirement and Ida having no source of income, they could no longer afford the large home on Grand Boulevard. Besides, except young Ida, all their children were married and out of the house. Ferdinand and Ida sold their home and moved with their daughter into a five-room apartment on Garfield Boulevard.

Sometime around March of 1931 Ida began what may have been intended as the final chapter of her autobiography. She called it "The Price of Liberty" and started the chapter with the words "Eternal vigilance is the price of liberty," a motto associated with Thomas Jefferson. In this chapter she evidently intended to describe how talking about equality wasn't enough. People had to back up their talk with action.

A new organization called the American Citizenship Federation had been established. Its purposes included the promotion of racial harmony, and as a result the federation attracted both black and white members. One of its goals was to build a peace temple in Chicago dedicated to the ideals of liberty and equality and modeled after Philadelphia's Independence Hall, where the Declaration of Independence had been adopted. To help raise the two million dollars needed to construct the peace temple, the organization planned to hold a big fundraising dinner at a Chicago hotel on George Washington's birthday.

At first both black and white people were to be invited to the dinner, but the hotel sent word that it would not serve black guests. Instead of moving the dinner elsewhere, the federation's white leaders agreed to make it a whites-only affair. However, Robert S. Abbott, owner and publisher of the *Chicago Defender,* was mistakenly sent an invitation and responded that he would be there.

A messenger from the federation called on Mr. Abbott to inform him that the hotel staff would not serve him and that it would cause quite a scene if he showed up as the only black guest at the dinner. Mr. Abbott was said to have answered that he understood the situation and would not attend the whites-only dinner. To show that he had no hard feelings, Mr. Abbott reportedly promised to contribute $10,000 to the federation (equal to $100,000 today).

When she heard that black people were excluded from the fundraising dinner, Ida B. Wells-Barnett was furious. She led a delegation of black American Citizenship Federation members to visit the organization's executive secretary. She minced no words and demanded to know if the organization had really gone along with the hotel's policy of excluding blacks. When he admitted it, she told him, "The time to put into practice the ideals you profess is at hand. If you start in by condoning the race prejudice which meets us everywhere, the American Citizenship Federation is no different from other organizations, all of which lay down this color line."

Ida withdrew from the organization, visited Mr. Abbott to criticize his accepting the insult, and wrote accounts of the matter for Chicago newspapers, blasting the hotel for its bigotry. In addition, she sent letters to all thirty-three members of the American Citizenship Federation's board of directors, informing them about the bigotry allowed by their so-called integrated organization. Several members of the board of directors sent her letters in response. She was just about to describe these letters in her autobiography when she left off not only in the middle of a sentence but in the middle of a word:

> I also received some beautiful letters from members of the
> board of directors thanking us for calling attention to what
> was go

Those were the last words the Princess of the Press would ever write. On Saturday, March 21, 1931, Ida went downtown to shop. That evening she complained of not feeling well. She spent the next day in bed. By Monday morning Ida was barely conscious. Her family rushed her to the hospital, but the doctors could not save her.

On March 25, 1931, the thirty-fifth birthday of her oldest child, Charles, Ida B. Wells-Barnett died of uremic poisoning, a condition associated with kidney disease, at the age of sixty-eight. Born a slave, she had spent most of her life battling to end lynching, segregation, and

Ida B. Wells-Barnett in her later years

other injustices. Famous people sang her praises. W. E. B. Du Bois called her "the pioneer of the anti-lynching crusade in the United States" who "began the awakening of the conscience of the nation." Others praised her "uncompromising stand against inequality" and called her "one of the few voices of protest" of her time.

But the tribute that she herself had treasured most was a letter from a poor Mississippi sharecropper who had mailed her a dollar to help her anti-lynching crusade. "The only thing to offer for you in your great undertaking [is] prayer," he had written, "and this goes up from every lip. The words GOD BLESS HER is written here on every acre of ground, and on every doorstep, and inside of every home."

The Legacy of Ida B. Wells-Barnett

FERDINAND LEE BARNETT, Ida's husband of thirty-six years, practiced law until he was close to eighty years old. He might have worked even longer, but the Great Depression that began in 1929 and lasted ten years cost him and millions of other people their jobs. Ferdinand died in 1936 at the age of eighty-four and was buried in Chicago's Oak Woods Cemetery alongside his wife. The headstone over their graves reads simply CRUSADERS FOR JUSTICE.

Meanwhile, Ida's achievements were falling into obscurity, although now and then there was a reminder of Ida B. Wells-Barnett. In 1940 a Chicago housing project was named the Ida B. Wells Homes in her honor. In 1950 Chicago named her one of the greatest women in its nearly two-hundred-year history. But like the young woman who asked her, "Won't you please tell me what it was you did?" most Americans had, at best, only a vague idea of who she was. The autobiography that would have answered this question sat gathering dust, for no publisher had sufficient interest in bringing it out.

Although lynching had been nearly wiped out by the time of Wells-Barnett's death, segregation continued virtually unchanged until the 1950s, especially in the South. Then a new generation of black and white Americans who possessed Wells-Barnett's sense of justice and crusading spirit began to change the laws of the land. They helped pass the Civil Rights Act of 1964, which outlawed employment discrimination and segregation in public and private places; the Voting Rights Act of 1965, which assured black people of their right to the ballot; and the Open Housing Act of 1968, which outlawed discrimination in the sale or rental of housing.

As these changes occurred, black studies became an important subject in our nation's schools. Children learned about Rosa Parks, who in 1955 refused to give up her seat to a white bus passenger in Montgomery, Alabama, and about Dr. Martin Luther King Jr., who led nonviolent opposition to segregation and discrimination. They also learned about other prominent black people: Jackie Robinson, the first black major-league baseball player; Richard Wright, author of the powerful novel *Native Son;* George Washington Carver, a plant scientist who made soap, ink, and other products from peanuts; Louis Armstrong, the one-of-a-kind jazz trumpeter and singer; and Thurgood Marshall, the first black justice of the U.S. Supreme Court.

But Ida B. Wells-Barnett was largely forgotten. This was partly because her achievements had occurred so long ago. When she died, Martin Luther King Jr. was only two years old. Also, Wells-Barnett was a woman, and with such notable exceptions as Harriet Tubman and Rosa Parks, men were the focus of attention at first in black studies. Besides, Ida's crusade was so successful that most children today don't even know the meaning of the word *lynching.*

Then in the 1960s and 1970s the women's rights movement gained momentum. Black women began to research the women of long ago who laid the groundwork for the modern civil rights movement. They rediscovered Ida B. Wells-Barnett and elevated her to her rightful place in history. Thirty-nine years after Wells-Barnett's death, her daughter Alfreda M. Barnett Duster found a publisher for *Crusade for Justice,* the great civil rights leader's autobiography. The book was published in 1970, when Alfreda was sixty-six years old, nearly the age her mother had been when she died. Four years later, in 1974, the U.S. Department

Ida B. Wells-Barnett's home on Grand Boulevard (now Martin Luther King Drive)

of the Interior designated Ida B. Wells-Barnett's Grand Boulevard home a National Historic Landmark.

The book that did the most to introduce Wells-Barnett to college students was Dorothy Sterling's *Black Foremothers: Three Lives*. First published in 1979, it offers sketches of Wells-Barnett, her sometime friend Mary Church Terrell, and Ellen Craft, who escaped slavery by fleeing to the North disguised as a man. Ten years later, in 1989, PBS aired a memorable television documentary, *Ida B. Wells: A Passion for Justice*. Her face became familiar to millions of people when the nation issued an Ida B. Wells postage stamp for its Black Heritage series in 1990. Amid all the renewed interest in her, *The Memphis Diary of Ida B. Wells* was published in 1995, and several biographies about her for children also appeared during the 1990s. The Ida B. Wells High School in San Francisco honors her memory, and the University of Kansas issues a yearly award named

Ida B. Wells stamp

Ida B. Wells

25
Black Heritage USA

for her. The Ida B. Wells Award honors people who have worked to hire and promote minorities in the news media. The recipient receives a plaque and a sculpture of Wells-Barnett created by University of Kansas artist Elden C. Tefft.

Ida B. Wells-Barnett would have enjoyed this recognition, but the progress made in civil rights issues would have given her far more pleasure. Yet if she were alive today, she would undoubtedly say that we have a long way to go before our country offers equality and justice for all. Like her autobiography, which broke off in the middle of a word, the crusade for justice for which she struggled all her life remains unfinished.

Bibliography

Capers, Gerald M. *The Biography of a River Town.* Chapel Hill, N.C.: University of North Carolina Press, 1939.

Douglass, Frederick. *Narrative of the Life of Frederick Douglass.* New York: New American Library, 1968.

Du Bois, W. E. B. *The Souls of Black Folk.* London: A. Constable, 1905.

Freedman, Suzanne. *Ida B. Wells-Barnett and the Antilynching Crusade.* Brookfield, Conn.: Millbrook Press, 1994.

Hamilton, William Baskerville. *Holly Springs, Mississippi, to the Year 1878.* Holly Springs, Miss.: Marshall County Historical Society, 1984.

Holt, Thomas C. "The Lonely Warrior: Ida B. Wells-Barnett and the Struggle for Black Leadership" from *Black Leaders of the Twentieth Century.* Franklin, John Hope, and August Meier, eds. Urbana, Ill.: University of Illinois Press, 1982.

Klots, Steve. *Ida Wells-Barnet.* New York: Chelsea House, 1994.

McIlwaine, Shields. *Memphis Down in Dixie.* New York: E. P. Dutton, 1948.

National Association for the Advancement of Colored People. *Thirty Years of Lynching in the United States: 1889–1918.* New York: Arno Press and the New York Times, 1969.

Penn, I. Garland. *The Afro-American Press and Its Editors.* Springfield, Mass.: Wiley & Co., 1891.

Raper, Arthur F. *The Tragedy of Lynching*. Chapel Hill, N.C.: University of North Carolina Press, 1933.

Sterling, Dorothy. *Black Foremothers: Three Lives*, 2nd ed. New York: Feminist Press, 1988.

Van Steenwyk, Elizabeth. *Ida B. Wells-Barnett: Woman of Courage*. New York: Franklin Watts, 1992.

Wells-Barnett, Ida B. *The Arkansas Race Riot*.

———. *Crusade for Justice: The Autobiography of Ida B. Wells*. Alfreda M. Barnett Duster, ed. Chicago: University of Chicago Press, 1970.

———. *Lynch Law in Georgia*. Chicago: Privately printed by "Chicago colored citizens," 1899.

———. *The Memphis Diary of Ida B. Wells*. Miriam DeCosta-Willis, ed. Boston: Beacon Press, 1995.

———. *Selected Works of Ida B. Wells-Barnett* (reprints of *Southern Horrors: Lynch Law in All Its Phases; The Reason Why the Colored American Is Not in the World's Columbian Exposition; A Red Record;* and *Mob Rule in New Orleans*). New York: Oxford University Press, 1991.

White, Walter. *Rope and Faggot: A Biography of Judge Lynch*. New York: Arno Press and the New York Times, 1969.

Woodward, C. Vann. *The Strange Career of Jim Crow*, 2nd rev. ed. New York: Oxford University Press, 1966.

Video: William Greaves Productions. *Ida B. Wells: A Passion for Justice*. Alexandria, Virginia: PBS Video, 1989.

Picture Credits

The photographs in this book are from the following sources and are used by permission and through the courtesy of the copyright owners:

Arkansas History Commission: pages 3, 157

Atlanta Journal and *Atlanta Constitution:* pages 114, 115

Chicago Historical Society: page 154

Alfreda Barnett Duster Family: pages xiv, 99, 134, 168

Alfreda Duster Ferrell: page 125

Judith Bloom Fradin: pages 83, 99, 114, 115, 134, 167

Library of Congress: pages ii, xi, 6, 8, 11, 12, 18, 29, 40, 47, 47, 51, 52, 59, 64, 65, 78, 89, 91, 95, 106, 109, 112, 121, 127, 132, 139, 143, 158, 160, 172

Marshall County (Mississippi) Museum: pages 7, 10

Memphis/Shelby County Public Library & Information Center: pages 14, 24, 31

National Association for the Advancement of Colored People: page 83

North Wind Picture Archives: pages 71, 98, 102

Schomburg Center for Research in Black Culture, The New York Public Library: pages 22, 26, 28, 55, 62, 141

University of Chicago Library, Department of Special Collections: pages viii, 35, 42, 45, 66, 75, 101, 122, 146, 148, 163

Index

Note: Page numbers in **bold** type refer to illustrations.